Great Britain Geological Survey

Explanation of Sheet 31

Stirling (southern part), Lanarkshire (northern part), Linlithgowshire

(western borders)

Great Britain Geological Survey

Explanation of Sheet 31
Stirling (southern part), Lanarkshire (northern part), Linlithgowshire (western borders)

ISBN/EAN: 9783337343668

Printed in Europe, USA, Canada, Australia, Japan

Cover: Foto ©Andreas Hilbeck / pixelio.de

More available books at **www.hansebooks.com**

Memoirs of the Geological Survey,

SCOTLAND.

EXPLANATION OF SHEET
31.

STIRLING (SOUTHERN PART).
LANARKSHIRE (NORTHERN PART).
LINLITHGOWSHIRE (WESTERN BORDERS).

EDINBURGH:
PRINTED FOR HER MAJESTY'S STATIONERY OFFICE,
AND SOLD BY
W. & A. K. JOHNSTON, 4 ST ANDREW SQUARE;
ALSO IN LONDON BY
STANFORD, 6 CHARING CROSS, W.C.; LETTS & SON, ROYAL EXCHANGE, E.C.;
LONGMAN & Co., PATERNOSTER ROW; AND WYLD, 11 AND 12 CHARING CROSS;
AND IN DUBLIN BY
HODGES, FOSTER, & Co., 104 GRAFTON STREET.
1 8 7 9.

Price 2s. 3d.]

PREFACE.

THE Map of which the following pages are an explanation embraces the richest mineral district of central Scotland—the great Lanarkshire and Stirlingshire coalfields stretching between Glasgow, Grangemouth, and Bathgate. The general geological structure of this area has long been known, and numerous descriptive papers have been published regarding different parts of it, of which the more important will be found enumerated at the close of this Explanation. No detailed map of it, however, has preceded the present Sheet of the Geological Survey, in which, for the first time, the coals, ironstones, and limestones, with their sinuous outcrops and numerous faults, are delineated, and the area and structure of the surrounding older formations are correctly traced.

The survey of Sheet 31 was begun by myself as far back as the year 1858, under the directorship of the late Sir Roderick I. Murchison. Owing to the defective condition of the Ordnance Survey Maps, however, it was found impossible at that time to carry the geological mapping further west than the limits of Linlithgowshire, and the work of the Geological Survey had to be transferred to other districts. The examination of the great Scottish coalfield was commenced from the south-west side, where the Ayrshire Maps were available, and the work proceeded across the country under the directorship of Professor A. C. Ramsay, until at last the lines were joined up with those which had been traced nearly twenty years before.

The mapping of Sheet 31 has been the work of Mr E. Hull, F.R.S. (now director of the Geological Survey of Ireland), Mr James Geikie, F.R.S., Mr B. N. Peach, Mr R. L. Jack, and myself, each having his own area, and working with my co-operation. Mr Hull, while mapping the area around Glasgow, carried his lines into the present Map along the strip of ground extending with a breadth of more than a mile, from the Cathkin Hills northwards to the valley of the Kelvin. Mr J. Geikie surveyed the remainder and much the larger part of Lanarkshire, his area extending over about two-fifths of the Sheet, from its southern edge up to the borders of Dumbartonshire and Stirlingshire, and into the south-western part of Linlithgowshire as far as Armadale, Torbanehill, Whitburn, and Hendrey's Course. Mr Peach took the area lying to the west of Linlithgowshire and north of Lanarkshire, and extending westwards a little beyond Kilsyth. Mr Jack's portion embraced the rest of the north-west district of the Map from Cadder and Kirkintilloch north to Fintry, and included the larger part of the Campsie Hills. The Linlithgowshire ground, with the exception of the part above referred to, was surveyed by me in connection with the area lying to the eastward (Sheet 32).

To the following Explanation Mr J. Geikie has contributed paragraphs 3, 7, 15, 22, 41, 56, 57, 59–68, 77, 78, 82, 84–89, 91, 93, 94, 96, 97, 99, 101, 102, 104, 107, 111, 112, 114, 116, 117, 120–123. Mr Peach Nos. 12, 19, 20, 42–49, 58, 69–76, 83, 90, 92, 95, 98, 100, 103, 105, 106, 108, 109, 110, 113, 115, 118, 119, 124–128. Besides editing the whole, I have supplied paragraphs 1, 2, 4, 5, 6, 8, 9, 10, 11, 13, 14, 16, 17, 18, 21, 23–40, 50–56, 79–81. Since he completed the survey of his area in Sheet 31, Mr Jack has been appointed Government Geologist in Queensland. I have supplied the description of that area from his maps and notes, supplemented by my own memoranda made when inspecting the ground with him.

The Fossil Lists in the Appendix and throughout the Explanation have been prepared by Mr Robert Etteridge, jun., by whom the fossils have been determined.

GEOLOGICAL SURVEY OFFICE,   ARCH. GEIKIE.
    EDINBURGH, *Oct.* 1878.

EXPLANATION OF SHEET 31.

I. AREA EMBRACED IN THE MAP.

1. The present Sheet of the Geological Survey of Scotland embraces an area of 432 square miles, lying within the most populous and important counties of central Scotland. Its western margin traverses the eastern suburbs of Glasgow, and runs northward across the Campsie Fells to the village of Fintry. Its eastern limits are marked by the chain of heights which extend from Borrowstounness, by Linlithgow, to Bathgate and the moorlands, which swell southwards into the eminences of Hendrey's Course and Levenseat. On the north it extends to beyond Larbert, and takes in about five miles of the course of the River Forth, above Borrowstounness. On the south it cuts across the great Clyde coal-field from the Cathkin Hills by Bothwell and Motherwell to the uplands of Levenseat. It thus embraces the greater part of the Lanarkshire and Stirlingshire mineral fields, a portion of the carse-lands of the Forth, the pastoral tracts of the Kilsyth and Campsie or Fintry Hills, with the populous centres of Airdrie, Coatbridge, Slamannan, Kirkintilloch, Kilsyth, Falkirk, Linlithgow, Borrowstounness, and Bathgate.

II. FORM OF THE GROUND.

2. Seen from the top of one of the neighbouring heights—such, for example, as one of the range of the Kilsyth Hills—the area shown upon the map appears as a broad undulating plain, rising almost imperceptibly from the north, until it loses itself among the southern moorlands. This plain probably does not exceed 500 feet in average elevation. At its northern end it sinks to the sea-level at the estuary of the Forth. On the east it is bounded by the range of the Bathgate Hills, which rise conspicuously to a height of 1000 feet above the sea. Towards the north-west, its margin is still more sharply defined by the Kilsyth Hills, which tower above it in a line of steep escarpment, reaching in some places a height of more than 1700 feet above the sea, and fully 1300 feet above the low ground at its base. At the south-west corner of the Map a portion of the heights is shown which border the edge of the plain on that quarter. To the southward, the low undulating country stretches up the vale of Clydesdale, but rises in the central and eastern parts of the plain into wide morass-covered moors, which, to the south of Slamannan, attain heights of from 600 to 900 feet.

3. This Sheet affords abundant examples of the connection between external forms of the ground and geological structure. Where, for instance, hard and softer rocks come together, the former, as is well known, generally project above the level of the latter. In this way the patches of

igneous rock, which are scattered all over the area included in the Map, never fail to give rise to hills and knolls, save where the whole ground is deeply buried under superficial accumulations of clay, sand, or other loose materials. On the other hand, the sedimentary formations, though they sometimes form elevated tracts of country, as in the moors about Leven-seat and Hendrey's Course, do not of themselves stand out as prominent and picturesque features of the landscape, like the rugged hills, crags, and knolls of the igneous masses. The valleys do not necessarily coincide in direction with *faults*, since these latter cross valleys and hills alike, and only show at the surface of the ground when they happen to have brought hard and soft rocks together, in which case the superficial inequality is due entirely to the relative degree of denudation which the unequally yielding rocks have experienced, and not to any vertical displacement. This is well shown when the ground along what is geologically the *low* side of a fault, instead of being depressed below the level of the ground on the *high* side, actually overlooks it.

4. Besides the general influence of denudation in producing inequalities of surface, owing to the different powers of resistance of the various kinds of rock, a further examination of the Map will show that there has been a widespread influence at work in producing a series of parallel ridges and hollows, which are not confined to any one kind of rock, but traverse all the rock masses, even the hardest and most prominent. These features are expressed by the shading on the Map, from which their general direction will be seen to run from W.S.W. to E.N.E. It will be shown on a subsequent page that they are greatly due to the manner in which the drift deposits have been arranged, and that their trend coincides with that of the ice striæ on the rocks. But, as may be seen among the hills to the south of Linlithgow, they are well marked among the hard igneous rocks, and traverse these even at right angles to the strike of their beds. Such a system of harmonious surface grooving could not possibly result from the influence of so varied a geological arrangement of rocks as is shown upon the Map, but must be attributed to a superficial agent, moving across the country in an easterly direction.

5. There are some portions of this district where these remarkable features in the form of the ground are especially well developed, and where all their characteristics can be studied within a limited and easily accessible compass. Such is the tract of Stirlingshire and the west of Linlithgow-shire, lying to the south of the line of the Edinburgh and Glasgow Railway. To the south of Falkirk, the ground undulates in a series of long parallel ridges and hollows, rising in places to a height of between 600 and 700 feet, and uniformly directed towards E.N.E. From the sinuous outcrops of the coal-seams, it is evident that these inequalities are due to actual erosion of the Carboniferous rocks, and that they are not affected by the faults which traverse the coal-field. Not only have the natural features of the surface been determined here by the general erosion from the west, so that the lakes, mosses, and water-courses run in the same uniform trend as the ridges which separate them, but the artificial features also, such as roads, ditches, plantations, and even the boundary walls between the fields, have their direction similarly defined by the prevailing character.

6. The watershed of Scotland, between the Atlantic Ocean and the North Sea, crosses the Map from north-west to south-east; the streams on the west side being tributaries of the Clyde, while those on the east side join the Forth. At the north-west corner of the Map a feature of this watershed is well exhibited by the approach of the rivers Endrick, which falls into Loch Lomond, and the Carron, which is a tributary of the Forth. The space between these streams is here a low

narrow flat valley, through which it would not be difficult to divert the Endrick and Carron rivers, the one into the other. Other examples of the same kind have been already described in former memoirs of the Geological Survey. One of the most remarkable is the approach of the Clyde and Tweed at either end of the valley of Biggar; another on a smaller scale, but in the same neighbourhood, is furnished by the Medwin Water and the Lyne. Passing round the sources of the River Carron, the watershed strikes east along the chain of the Kilsyth Hills to near Banton, where it descends into the plain, and turning round by Cumbernauld, winds southwards across the moors.

7. On the south-west side of this line, the most important streams are the River Clyde, with its tributaries, the Kelvin, the North, the South, and the Rotten Calder Waters. Only a small part of the Clyde is shown on the Map. This begins at the Hamilton Parks, and passes west by north to Rutherglen, where it leaves the Sheet. From that river the ground rises somewhat rapidly to the south (1 in 16 or so), attaining a height of 700 feet or thereabout, at the extreme south-west corner of the Sheet. Toward the north and north-east, the rise is much less considerable, the crest of the watershed between the Clyde and Forth being attained in the Moffat and Torrance Hills at a height of little more than 900 feet, and a distance of ten miles at least from the River Clyde, near Uddingston. A glance at the Map will show that north of a line, drawn from the left hand margin of the Map near Hogganfield Loch, east by Cardowan and Gartsherrie to the waterparting in the moors north-east of Airdrie, the ground falls away gently towards the valley of the Kelvin. South of the same line the slope is more or less directly into the valley of the Clyde. Most of the streams have cut deep gullies or ravines for themselves, either out of the superficial formations or out of the underlying rocks, or in many cases out of both. The gorge of the Clyde between Bothwell Bridge and Uddingston is the finest example; on a smaller scale the North and South Calder Waters afford many picturesque ravines, where the coal-measure strata are well exposed.

8. On the north-east side of the watershed the Carron river drains the high pastoral tract of the Kilsyth Hills, and after receiving the Bonny Water from the right, winds for the last seven or eight miles of its course through the flat alluvial land of the Forth known as the Carse of Falkirk. The Rivers Avon and Almond, and the Breich Water, with their upper feeders, rise among the mosses which cover the high moors on the watershed. On the whole these streams flow in shallow hollows, which they have worn out of the drift deposits. This feature is specially shown by the Almond and the Breich. Now and then the water has cut down into the rocks beneath, while, still more rarely, rocky and sometimes narrow and precipitous channels have been excavated. By much the best example is that of the gorge of the Avon between Muiravonside and Manuel. But the Carron for some miles above Denny flows in a picturesque, wooded, and rocky ravine.

9. As regards the vegetation, there are three well-marked forms of surface within the area of the present Map :—1st, Arable land, including ground covered with woods and plantations. The low tracts bordering the River Forth are very generally under the plough. Cultivation stretches westward along the base of the Kilsyth Hills and south to the vale of the Clyde, up which it extends, between the Cathkin and adjacent hills on the left bank and the high moors on the right. It likewise runs south along the slopes of the Bathgate Hills, but gradually diminishes as the ground rises into the bleak moory country between Whitburn and the heights of Hendrey's Course and Levenseat. On the arable land at all

elevations, as well as in some of the less sterile mossy tracts, considerable belts of wood have been planted. Thus, beginning close to the sea-level near Borrowstounness, plantations appear on some of the stiff clayey soil which is elsewhere devoted to crops; scattered clumps, chiefly of firs, are dotted over the ground as it rises into the Bathgate Hills, the very tops of that range of heights being wooded; while to the south and south-west, where the soil becomes cold and stiff, and the ground is high and bleak, long strips of wood have been made to grow. In the vale of the Clyde, where the rich alluvial soil and the sheltered situation favours their growth, the best woods in the district are to be seen. 2d, Moors, mosses, and boggy land. The high bleak parts of the plain, which rise from the valley of the Clyde and undulate eastwards and northwards, between Airdrie, Whitburn, and Falkirk, are essentially moors and peat-mosses. The slopes and ridges are covered with a heathy vegetation, which, in the hollows, passes into sheets of peat or undrained marshes. Cultivation and mining operations every year encroach more and more upon these wastes. Even in the arable tracts which have been long under the plough evidence may be found that marshes and peat-mosses once existed abundantly all over the country. The carse-land of the margin of the Forth was formerly covered with peat, though this has now in large measure been removed, and the good underlying clay soil brought into cultivation. Considerable areas of peat-moss still remain, as the Letham Moss to the north-east of Larbert. 3d, Pastoral tracts. The only extensive area of this kind is that of the Kilsyth and Fintry Hills. Formed of decomposing igneous rocks, which crumble rather into sloping declivities than into crags and cliffs, these heights are clothed even to their summits with pasture, while their height brings them within such an abundant rainfall as to preserve them well-watered.

10. III. FORMATIONS AND GROUPS OF ROCK EMBRACED BY THE MAP.

Aqueous.

Sign on Map.

Recent and Post-Tertiary,	Alluvium of river-terraces and old lakes, · · · Peat, · · ·	Freshwater,	~
	Recent mud of Forth, · · Lower raised beaches, · ·	Estuarine and marine,	~
Drift Series,	Sands, Gravels, and Stratified Clays of upper terrace of Forth and Clyde (estuarine and marine); · · · · ·	See Index on margin of Map.	
	Erratic Blocks, Sands, Gravels with Stratified Clays, Kame Series. Boulder Clays. River Deposits below Boulder Clay. Ice-markings on rocks, · · ·		⊖→
Carboniferous,	Upper Red Sandstone Group, without Coal, · ·		d⁶
	Coal Measures, · · · · · ·		d⁵
	Millstone Grit, · · · · ·		d⁴
	Carboniferous Limestone Series, · · ·		d²
	Calciferous Sandstone Series, · · · ·		d¹, d¹'

Igneous.

a: *Interbedded, or contemporaneous with the formations among which they lie.*

In Carboniferous,	Basalt, Dolerite, (Diabase), in lava beds, ·	Bd
	Volcanic Tuff, · · · ·	Fsd
	Porphyrite, in lava beds, · · ·	Fd

b. *Intrusive, or subsequent in date to the formations in which
they are found.*

Of Miocene (?) Age.	Basalt-rocks in dykes, ...	B
,, Post-Carboniferous Age.	Basalt in intrusive sheets, .	B
	Basalt, ...	B
,, Lower Carboniferous,	Felstone, . . .	F
	Agglomerate . . .	N

IV. GEOLOGICAL STRUCTURE OF THE DISTRICTS INCLUDED WITHIN THE MAP.

11. Disregarding minor features, the area embraced within the Map may be looked upon as a long basin, the centre of which runs from south to north, or rather from S.S.W. to N.N.E. Along the centre of this trough lie the higher members of the Carboniferous system, forming the coal-fields of Carron, Falkirk, Slamannan, Shotts, Airdrie, and Mother-well. Along the eastern margin a continuous belt of the sandstones known as the Millstone Grit rises from underneath the Coal-measures, followed in turn by a broad band of the Carboniferous Limestone series with its associated volcanic rocks. From below this series the Calciferous Sandstones emerge to the surface, a small area of them being included in the Map to the east and south-east of Bathgate. The western side of the trough is much less regular. Beginning at the north end, we find the two parallel bands of Millstone Grit and Carboniferous Limestone well developed between the Kilsyth Hills and Larbert. Owing, however, to a succession of minor outlying basins and of large faults, the true trough-shaped structure of the whole area is apt to be missed on that side.

12. A better idea may be formed from the Map of the more complex character of the structure of the ground on this side than can be given by a description. It will there be seen how the edge of the Coal-measures is shifted successively further west by the long parallel east and west faults ; how these faults likewise affect the continuity of the boundary-lines of the Millstone Grit and Limestone series ; and how, owing to undulations of the dip, as well as to dislocations, portions of these sandstones are brought in as isolated patches or outliers. It is between the valley of the Carron and Kirkintilloch that these features are best developed. In that tract the Carboniferous strata flanking the Kilsyth Hills have been thrown into a series of small basins and domes often greatly broken by faults. The most remarkable result of these irregularities of structure is probably to be found in the strip of ground which includes the Coney-park, Banknock, and Dennyloanhead coal-fields. A narrow strip of Coal-measures is there found wedged in between two faults, which converge and unite westwards and open out to the east. By means of these dislo-cations much higher parts of the coal-measures than any found in the main Stirlingshire coal-field are let down and preserved between beds of the Carboniferous Limestone series on the one side and a higher portion of the same series and the Millstone Grit on the other. To the strip of coal-measures thus let in among older strata a narrow and deep basin-shape has been given. The Banton and Kilsyth coal-fields form a series of little basins in the Carboniferous Limestone series, wherein the same beds are constantly repeated. Such a succession of basins implies a corre-sponding number of saddles or domes. Of these the most noteworthy in the district is that which extends from the station on the Roman wall about a mile and a half west from Croy, on the Edinburgh and Glasgow Railway, for 3 miles to the north-east to Low Banton. This one is so conspicuous that it has acquired the local name of the "riggin" or roof.

13. On the western margin of the coal-fields a feature is well displayed, which occurs not infrequently in Ayrshire and Lanarkshire. Higher portions of the Carboniferous system are there brought down by faults against the volcanic masses which lie not far above the base of that system. On the left bank of the Clyde, as shown at the south-west corner of the Map, the Coal-measures, and even the upper red sandstones, the very highest zone of the whole of the Carboniferous subdivisions, has been thrown against the porphyrites of the Cathkin Hills which overlook all the plain to the north and east. The flanks of the Kilsyth Hills are likewise everywhere bounded by one or more faults, whereby various horizons of the Carboniferous Limestone series are brought down against the base of the steep volcanic escarpment. So sinuous is the line of displacement in some parts of its course that the Limestone series seems as it were notched into the older igneous base. Possibly this character may have partly contributed to the mistaken notion which prevailed until recently, that the igneous rocks of the Campsie and Kilsyth Hills were later in date than, and had invaded and overlaid, the Carboniferous Limestone of their faults. Reference may be made to Sheet 22 of the Geological Survey of Scotland for a still more striking illustration of this geological structure along the base of the hills between Ardrossan and Lochwinnoch.

14. More detailed reference will be made in the sequel to these and the other faults in the area of the Map. From the number and extent of the crimson and scarlet patches and bands upon the Map, it will be seen how abundant are the igneous rocks. Reserving detailed descriptions for a later section of this Explanation, we may here note that two great groups of volcanic masses, including lavas and tuffs, are here intercalated in the Carboniferous rocks. The older of these lies in the Calciferous Sandstone series, and forms the Kilsyth Hills on the north-west, and the Cathkin Hills on the south-west. The younger series is interbedded with the Carboniferous Limestone series, and extend from Borrowstounness southwards by Linlithgow and Bathgate to Blackburn. Many intrusive sheets of basalt and dolerite have been injected into the Carboniferous Limestone, Millstone Grit, and Coal-measures, particularly along the central parts of the basin from Torphichen to Glasgow, and on its north-western margin between Kirkintilloch and the hills above Dunipace, which stretch on to Stirling. Later still than most, perhaps than all of these intrusions, are the long parallel east and west dykes which cross indifferently all the rocks, both aqueous and igneous.

In the following description of the geological structure of this area, the rocks of each formation are described in ascending order, beginning with the oldest, and their area and arrangement are traced across the districts into which, for the sake of convenience, the area has been divided.

Carboniferous.

15. Underneath the various superficial deposits to be afterwards described, the whole of the rocks of this area, with the exception of some of the intrusive igneous sheets and dykes, belong to the Carboniferous system. All the great subdivisions of that system in Scotland are represented here. Their arrangement, and the localities upon the Map where they may be examined, are shown in the annexed table.

Sign on Map.	Groups of Strata.	Localities.
d⁵′	**Coal-measures,** consisting of— (*b*). Red and grey sandstones, fireclays, shales, marls, etc., with Carboniferous plants. No workable coal-seams in this group.	River Clyde, between Bothwell and Carmyle; ravines of Luggie Burn from Langloan downwards, and of North Calder Water near Hagg Mill, and from Rosehall downwards; Rotten Calder; Bellshill; Bothwell; Uddingston; Carmyle; Shettleston; Baillieston; Drumpark, etc. A small outlier occurs in centre of Coneypark basin, as shown by mining operations. It is nowhere visible at the surface, and is the only representative of the subdivision in Stirlingshire.
d⁵	(*a*). A thick group of white and grey sandstones, dark shales, oil-shales, fireclays, coal-seams, and ironstones.	South Calder Water; North Calder Water down to Rosehall; tributaries of North Calder; River Avon, for 3½ miles down from Avonbridge; Slamannan, Falkirk, Carron, Coneypark, and Banknock coal-fields.
d⁴	**Millstone-Grit,** consisting of— A suite of massive, though lenticular sandstones and grits, with thick beds of fireclay, thin limestones, and occasional thin coals and ironstones.	River Avon, from Avonbank to Inveravon, and above Caribber; Whitburn; Levenseat and Gladsmuir Hills; near Salsburgh, Steps, Garnkirk; Heathfield, Glenboig, etc.; western boundary of Falkirk coal-field, where, though no good continuous natural sections occur, the sandstones rise into bare knobby hills from Fannyside Moor to Torwood Hill.
d²	**Carboniferous Limestone Series,** consisting of— (*c*). A group of three or more limestones, with coals, and thick beds of sandstone, etc.	Kinneil; Avon Water, between Avonbank and Easter Caribber; Bowden Hill; Stand Hill; Levenseat; Torwood; Denny; Castlecary; Cumbernauld; Mollinburn; Robroyston.
	(*b*). A group of sandstones, shales, etc., with beds of coal and ironstone; no limestone.	South of Hendrey's Course; Blaw Weary; Breich Water at Stonyburn; Bathgate; Borrowstounness; Denny; Banton; Kilsyth.
	(*a*). A group of sandstones, shales, etc., with several thick seams of limestone, and some coals, and ironstones. In Linlithgowshire (Bathgate Hills, to Borrowstounness) thick beds of contemporaneous basalt and tuff are associated with the Limestone series.	Addiewell; Bathgate Hills; Conie Burn, near Kilsyth; Lennoxtown; Carron Water, above Denny.

Sign on Map.	Groups of Strata.	Localities.
d¹ʳ	**Calciferous Sandstone Series,** consisting of— (*b*). Cement-stone group. On the eastern edge of the Map this group, consisting of white sandstones and black shales, comes out repeatedly underneath the Carboniferous Limestone series. On the north-west and at the south-west corner, however, it is represented by a thick mass of interbedded volcanic rocks (porphyrites, tuffs, &c.). Towards the top of this volcanic zone, in the Kilsyth Hills, blue, green, and red clays, and a few sandstone bands occur; while towards its base similar clays, with bands of cement-stone, and sandstone are interstratified. These strata thus resemble parts of the cement-stone group in the west of Scotland.	Breich Water, east from Addiewell; River Almond, below Blackburn. Kilsyth and Fintry Hills; good sections, abundant, particularly along the southern escarpment; and in the watercourses; and Cathkin Hills.
d¹	(*a*). A group of red, yellow, and variegated sandstones, with red and green sandy clays, with one thin band of interbedded porphyrite.	Garvel Burn and tributaries; Tackmadoun Burn; both near Kilsyth.

CALCIFEROUS SANDSTONE SERIES.

16. This lowest member of the Carboniferous system in Scotland is everywhere separable into two distinct groups. Of these, the lower, consisting almost wholly of red sandstone, retains a great similarity of character from the coast of Berwickshire to the shores of Argyleshire. Sometimes, indeed, it is absent, and then the upper group, or even the base of the second member of the system, the Carboniferous Limestone, comes to lie directly upon an older set of formations. The upper group, commonly termed the Cement-stone group, offers far greater variety of lithological characters and of thickness. Disregarding the numerous minor local changes in these respects, we can recognise two well-marked types for this group which, from their distribution across the country, may be known as the western or Clyde type, and the eastern or Forth type. In the former case the strata consist mainly of grey, blue, lilac, and red shales and clays, with courses, or even thick zones of white, grey, or yellow, sometimes reddish, sandstones, and bands and nodules of cement-stone. On the whole the rocks of this type are singularly unfossiliferous. They occur throughout Ayrshire and the basin of the Clyde, stretching eastwards to Stirling, and even partially re-appearing at the extreme western margin of Fife. They are likewise well developed in

Berwickshire, and with some remarkable variations in Roxburghshire and Dumfriesshire, whence they pass across the border, and show themselves in rapidly diminishing proportions at the base of the Scar Limestone series of Cumberland. This may be regarded therefore as the more frequent and characteristic aspect of the strata between the red sandstone below, and the bottom of the Carboniferous Limestone above. The eastern or Forth type is confined to the basin of the Firth of Forth. It extends from the centre of Linlithgowshire to the northern edge of Berwickshire, and throughout the county of Fife. The strata here consist chiefly of white and yellow (very rarely, and only towards the base, red) sandstones, blue and black shales, clay ironstones in bands and nodules, with occasional entomostracan, mytiloid or encrinal limestones, and some bands of coal. These rocks are usually as marked by the abundance of their fossil contents as the rocks of the Clyde type are distinguished for their barrenness in this respect. In some districts the chief fossils are plants, such as ferns (*Sphenopteris*, &c.); lepidodendroid forms, calamites, &c. With these are commonly associated abundant remains of *Leperditia* or other ostracods, and scales, teeth and coprolites of such ganoids as *Rhizodus, Megalichthys, Eurynotus*, &c. Such groupings of organic remains appear to point to fluviatile or at least estuarine conditions of deposit. But at various horizons, throughout even these apparently fresh or brackish-water formations, there occur bands of shale or limestone, with such unequivocally marine forms as crinoids, *Spirorbis, Edmondia, Mytilus, Aviculopecten, Bellerophon,* and *Orthoceras.*

The present Map includes an area within which occur small tracts of both these types of the Calciferous Sandstone series. The characters of the Forth beds are seen in the Linlithgowshire district; those of the Clyde or western type in the Kilsyth and Fintry Hills. At the south-west corner of the Map the Cathkin Hills likewise belong to the western type.

a. LINLITHGOWSHIRE DISTRICT.

17. On the eastern margin of the Map a small space is occupied by the upper part of this series between Addiewell and the Bathgate Hills. The strata, partially exposed to view in the courses of the River Almond and Briech Water, consist of yellow and grey sandstone, black, blue, and grey shales, oil-shales, and thin seams and balls of clay-ironstone. They pass immediately under the Hurlet Limestone and coal lying at the bottom of the Carboniferous Limestone series. In the Almond section the crop of the Houston coal—a marked seam in the upper division (Cement-stone group) of the Calciferous Sandstones of Linlithgowshire—occurs almost exactly at the edge of the Map. Consequently, at Red House and southwards, this coal lies comparatively near the surface (30 fathoms and upwards). A higher band of oil-shale, known as Raeburn's Shale, which has been met with in bores to the northward, probably crops somewhere east from Hopefield Mills. The green clays or marls which lie above the Houston coal, and afford an excellent geological horizon in the district, are seen in the channel of the stream due south from Red House. Higher up, a band of green nodular felspathic tuff, derived from the trituration of some of the diabase-lavas of contemporaneous date, is cut through by the Almond at Hopefield Mills. It contains balls of hard flinty limestone, is flanked on the east by highly indurated fissile sandstone, dipping W.N.W. at 42°, and may perhaps be a portion of a volcanic neck connected, not with the Calciferous Sandstones, but with the later eruptions of the Limestone series. About 100 yards further west, among some shales which dip westward up the stream, a thin seam of encrinite limestone occurs.

Similar thin bands, lying below the Hurlet Limestone, which is conveniently taken as the base of the Limestone series, are not uncommon in other parts of the Carboniferous region of Scotland. North from the Almond section the Calciferous Sandstones run up the east side of the Bathgate Hills. If, as will be explained on a later page, we take the Petershill or thick Bathgate limestone to be the Hurlet seam, then all the interstratified igneous sheets lying to the east will fall into the Calciferous Sandstone series. For the sake of continuity, however, these rocks will be described with the overlying igneous masses with which they are connected (par. 25 *et. seq.*). In the Breich Water section, as far as contained within the area of the Map, no strata so low in the series as the Houston coal occur. That seam crops out about a quarter of mile east from the point where the edge of the Map crosses the Breich Water. The upper oil-shale, which is worked at Addiewell, crops in this stream close to that point. It is overlaid by white and grey sandstone, and dark shales which pass below the Hurlet Limestone at Cuthill. In a stream between Blackburn Hall and Gardner's Hall another small exposure of these strata is to be seen. Among them occur some blue shales, with cement-stone and a thin seam of impure limestone.

b. KILSYTH AND FINTRY DISTRICT.

18. Both the lower or Red Sandstone group and the upper or Cement-stone group, into which the Calciferous Sandstone series of central Scotland is divided, are represented in this district under conditions which mark them as belonging distinctly to the western or Clyde type of development. The lower division consists of the usual red sandstones, and is seen only in two tracts within the area embraced by the Map, viz., near Kilsyth and at Fintry. The upper division partakes of the characters so widespread in northern Ayrshire, Renfrewshire, and Dumbartonshire. It is mainly made up of contemporaneously ejected volcanic masses, but here and there between the volcanic sheets, and overlying them, occur strata of grey and blue clay, shale and cement-stone, which present the usual characters of the western Cement-stone group. The volcanic rocks cover almost the whole of this district. The structure of the ground, as shown upon the Map, is comparatively simple. On the whole, the rocks dip towards the east, but at very low angles; so low, indeed, that in many places, particularly towards the eastern end of the Kilsyth Hills, they coincide in dip with the natural fall of the ground. The gently inclined volcanic beds rise above each other into the range of hills north of Kilsyth. Their southern front being short and steep, they present an escarpment of the porphyrite sheets on that side. On the northern side also, to the west of Fintry, a still more striking escarpment occurs. Owing to the easterly dip, these escarpments are highest towards the west, and gradually sink eastwards, until they pass underneath the overlying Carboniferous Limestone series. Hence the lower portions of the series can only be seen towards the base of the escarpments on the northern and southern sides of the hills. On the north a magnificent range of cliffs and rocky slopes stretches to the west of Fintry. These, however, do not come into the present Map; their description is reserved for the Explanation to accompany Sheet 30. It may be mentioned that on both sides of the valley of the River Endrick, below Fintry, the base of the volcanic series is seen to rest upon a thick mass of white sandstone, which in turn passes down into the ordinary red sandstones and shales which form the lower division of the Calciferous Sandstone series.

19. On the southern side of the Kilsyth Hills, immediately to the

north of the valley of Kilsyth, there rises from beneath the volcanic escarpment a strip of sloping ground, about three miles long by about one-third of a mile in its greatest breadth, in which, as shown upon the Map, the underlying red sandstones come to the surface. These strata here consist of red, yellow, and variegated sandstones, with red and green marls and a bed of concretionary cornstone. They peep out from under and dip beneath the overlying volcanic mass of the hills. Nowhere is their base visible, the edges of the lowest beds exposed being abruptly truncated by a large fault, whereby the overlying Carboniferous Limestone series is everywhere made to abut upon them. The coal-seams in the latter series are indeed wrought right up against them. It is important to note the great similarity between some of the sandstones of this group, especially the yellow ones, and many in the Carboniferous Limestone series to the south of the line of fault. This has often been adduced as evidence that the Kilsyth coals and ironstones underlie the volcanic rocks of the hills to the north, and that a fruitful coal-field lies yet unreached beneath that vast area of high ground. The sheets of intrusive basalt which are found above the coals and ironstone have also been confounded with the interbedded porphyrites of the Kilsyth Hills, which were unmistakably true lava-flows and ashes ejected at the surface, and buried under sediment long before the formation of the coal and ironstone seams of Kilsyth. Sufficient evidence is supplied by the present Map to show how erroneous is the impression that any workable coal-field can exist below the chain of the Campsie and Kilsyth Hills. Besides the evidence supplied by the character of the strata in the strip of underlying red sandstones now referred to, the section of the River Carron above Denny, as well as numerous similar exposures northwards to Stirling, show that the volcanic series passes conformably below the base of the Carboniferous Limestone series, in which the lowest workable coal-seams of the district occur. Again, on the north side of the hills, as already remarked in the preceding paragraph, the strata which emerge from underneath the volcanic cake of the Fells are shown by innumerable sections to belong to a series of rocks lower and older than even the base of the Carboniferous Limestone series. In the narrow strip of red sandstones to the north of Kilsyth, good sections are to be found in all the streamlets which descend the slopes. The best, however, occur in the Garrel Burn and its tributaries, where the beds on both sides of the large fault are exposed, and the relations of the red sandstones to the overlying porphyrites and tuffs are well seen. Two thin beds of decomposing slaggy and amygdaloidal porphyrite are found intercalated with the sandstones of this area.

20. The upper or Cement-stone group of the Calciferous Sandstones is mainly of volcanic origin in this district, being a prolongation of the great volcanic area of Ayrshire, Renfrewshire, and Dumbartonshire. It consists of a succession of slaggy porphyrites, separated by considerable thicknesses of well-bedded fine-grained tuffs. Two intercalations of sedimentary strata occur near the base of the volcanic masses, one consisting of red, green, and grey clays, with numerous bands of impure cement-stone and calcareous sandstone, the other of white sandstone. They are seen at the Garrel Burn and Berryhill, to the north of Kilsyth. These sedimentary rocks, with the igneous sheets between them, form a zone at least 400 feet thick. Above this is a constant succession of beds of porphyrite-lavas rising, bed above bed, for about 600 feet, with few or no intercalations of tuff, the beds being separated only by their own slaggy and brecciated upper and under surfaces. They show all grades of texture, from a compact hard, dark bluish-green rock, like a basalt, to a slaggy, earthy, purple porphyry, with large tabular crystals of felspar.

Some are dark grey, and contain sparsely set crystals of felspar, and sometimes grains of olivine. As a rule, the beds are thin and widespread. Overlying these old lava-flows, and exposed in sections along their eastern margin, occurs a series of blue, green, and red clays, which, towards its base, contains bands and nests of comminuted volcanic fragments. It is difficult to tell whether these point to a continuance of volcanic activity, or whether they are only derived by ordinary waste from the lava surfaces. South of the large fault spoken of as flanking the hills, two areas of volcanic tuff, belonging to the very highest part of the group, occur, and dip below the base of the Carboniferous Limestone. One is traversed by the Corrie Burn, about 2 miles W.N.W. from Kilsyth, and the other occurs to the north of the Banton coal-field. The tuffs in the former case contain intercalations of green sandstone, and a thick bed of ferruginous cement-stone, which, however, is much shattered from its proximity to the fault, and altered by an intersecting columnar basalt dyke. A circumstance deserving of remark in regard to the history of these ancient lavas and tuffs can be well observed within the area of the present Map, but still better by combining that area with the ground to the west and north. The total mass of volcanic material north of Kilsyth is about 1000 feet in vertical thickness. Further west it attains a still greater depth. When traced northwards, however (Sheet 39), it rapidly thins out towards Stirling, until at Causewayhead, about 1 mile north of that place, it has entirely disappeared. From these facts it is clearly seen that the volcanoes which supplied the lavas and tuffs lay not towards the north, but towards the west and south-west.

21. An interesting feature of the volcanic history of the district is the occurrence of numerous "necks," which represent some of the pipes or orifices from which the lavas and tuffs were emitted. These are more abundant and striking round the escarpment of the hills between Strathblane and Fintry. But some good illustrations occur upon the present Map. Of these the most conspicuous are the eminences of the Meikle Bin and Dungoil; another rises through the lower Red Sandstone north of Kilsyth. But several smaller patches occur, some of them, indeed, too small to find a place upon the one-inch Map. They are filled either with some kind of lava-form rock or with agglomerate, sometimes with both. When the rock is a consolidated lava, it usually has the characters of a felstone; is yellow or grey in colour, dull, sparingly porphyritic, but with scattered granules of quartz. Sometimes, as in Dungoil, it assumes more of the dark colour and granular texture of a dolerite. Similar rocks occur as intrusive dykes here and there throughout the hills. The agglomerate is dull grey or greenish in colour, varying in texture from a fine breccia up to a coarse tumultuous mass, with blocks so large that they seem at first rather to be portions of intrusive veins than actually erupted fragments. These characters are well shown upon Meikle Bin, where, on the summit, and again on the northern shoulder called Bin Bairn, old volcanic pipes occur. But the most remarkable of the extinct orifices of eruption, unlike the others, does not form a prominent hill; it lies in a great hollow of the hills between Dungoil and Meikle Bin, a little to the north of the summit level on the road between Campsie and Fintry. Good sections have been cut across the rocks of this vent both by the River Carron and by the Bin and Clachie Burns. In the Clachie Burn, below the turnpike road, some knobs of agglomerate are seen. But the same rock is better exposed in the bed of the Carron for nearly half a mile above the ford at Waterhead. In some places it is a coarse irregular agglomerate of the usual type found in the necks, but with a rather more crystalline matrix. At a short distance, however, from where it has this character, it becomes so crystalline and altered as to be hardly

recognisable, except by some of the sandstone or other blocks which have resisted the metamorphism. These sandstone fragments, however, have been converted into quartzite. Numerous small veins, of a pink or yellowish felstone, traverse the neck, and appear likewise in the ordinary bedded porphyrites which surround it, and through which it rises. In the Bin Burn, most of the channel, where it crosses this interesting area, flows in alluvium; but the same altered agglomerate is seen immediately above the alluvial plain, and it occupies some space in the bed of the Carron below the embouchure of the Bin Burn. Wherever sections have been cut by the streams into the surrounding porphyrites, these rocks are traversed by numerous veins of the pink or yellow felstone. There can be little doubt that we have here an important volcanic orifice of the Calciferous Sandstone period. Probably the crystalline altered aspect of the agglomerate is to be attributed to the prolonged ascent of steam and heated vapours after the actual explosions in the vent had ceased.

c. DISTRICT OF CATHKIN HILLS.

22. At the south-west corner of the Map another area of igneous rocks belonging to the Lower Calciferous series makes its appearance. These rocks consist of various kinds of porphyrite and melaphyre, arranged as regular bedded masses. Here and there they show thin intercalations of sandstone, grit, conglomeratic tuff, and tufaceous shale. They form a portion of the Carmunnock and Cathkin Hills, a general description of which has been given in the Memoir to accompany Sheet 23. The beds seem to dip at a low angle towards the south, and thus present an escarpment towards the north. They are everywhere cut off from the coalfields by faults.

Carboniferous Limestone Series.

23. This division of the Carboniferous system is well developed both on the eastern and western sides of the great synclinal trough, forming in each case a more or less regular band. On the east side the strike of the rocks continues so little varied, and is to so small an extent interrupted by serious dislocations, that the limestone belt can there be followed in a tolerably even line from the northern to the southern margin of the Map. On the west side, however, owing to the numerous undulations and faults already referred to, it has been greatly affected in its course. It is least disturbed, and presents more of its normal characters at the north end of the line, in the neighbourhood of Denny, where it runs north and south parallel with the Millstone Grit and Coal-measures, with a breadth of about two miles. South from the Carron, however, its breadth is so irregular, that while at Banton it hardly exceeds a mile, at Cumbernauld, two miles further south, it exceeds six miles, and again, near Lennoxtown, it diminishes to less than a mile and a half. The threefold subdivision, so characteristic of this series of strata in Scotland, is well marked throughout the area included within the Map,—1st, At the base lie some thicker limestones (three or more), notably the Hurlet limestone and coal, commonly taken as the basement bed of the whole series. These limestones are subordinate to sandstones and shales, and contain some coal-seams and ironstones; 2d, A thick group of sandstones, shales, fireclays, coal-seams, and ironstones. It is in this group that the chief coals and ironstones of the western and eastern collieries of the Map lie. 3d, An upper group of sandstones and shale, where some thinner limestones (usually three seams), with one or more thin coal-seams, are the most marked

B

strata. In describing the development of these groups across the ground it will be most convenient to parcel out the area into districts. (1.) The Eastern District may include the whole of the Carboniferous Limestone belt on the eastern margin of the Map. The western belt, owing to its irregularities, may be considered in separate districts, as—(2.) The Denny District, including that portion of the belt lying to the north of the Banknock and Dennyloanhead coal-field. (3.) The Cumbernauld and Kilsyth District, embracing the next section of the belt as far west as Kirkintilloch; and (4.) The Lennoxtown and Cadder District, including the remaining portion of the belt along the western edge of the Map.

a, THE EASTERN DISTRICT.

24. This long narrow belt naturally divides itself into three sections: —1st, The central volcanic tract of the Linlithgow and Bathgate Hills; 2d, The coal and limestone area to the north, including the western part of the Borrowstounness coal-field; 3d, The coal-bearing area to the south, including Bathgate, Blackburn, Stonyburn, and Levenseat.

25. (i.) *The Linlithgow and Bathgate Hills.*—In the Memoir to Sheet 32 a description has already been given of the structure of this range of high ground. To one who casually visits them these heights present so much irregularity of surface, and so many proofs of igneous action, that they may readily be supposed to possess a somewhat complicated geological structure. In reality, however, the igneous masses have not seriously disturbed the strike and order of the rocks. On the contrary, having been contemporaneously erupted as lava-streams and showers of volcanic dust, they have become interstratified with the limestone series, and have partaken with it in the movements by which its present dip, strike, and faulting have been produced. It will be observed from the Map that the limestone bands continue traceable through the hills, and that the general breadth of the belt there does not vary materially from that which it exhibits elsewhere, where, with a similar angle of inclination, no igneous rocks occur. In short, in the area of these volcanic hills various lavas and tuffs take the place of what would otherwise have been ordinary sandstones, shales, &c.

26. Beginning beneath the base of the series, we find, as before remarked, the upper portions of the Calciferous Sandstones coming out from beneath the igneous rocks of the hills to the east of Bathgate. As shown in Sheet 32, there is ample evidence that volcanic action had long been rife in this area before the time of the Carboniferous limestones. The lower lava-sheets to the east of the Petershill Lime Quarries (for the reason referred to in par. 17) may be assigned to the age of the Calciferous Sandstone series. These consist of varieties of basalt, varying in texture from a compact black fine-grained rock to pale greenish earthy amygdaloid. They occur in beds sometimes separated only by the more slaggy portions at the top and bottom of each flow, sometimes by thin layers of a dirty green granular tuff, evidently derived from the trituration of such a rock as the green earthy amygdaloid. At the Kirkton Lime Quarries two seams of limestone, with associated shales and tuffs, are interstratified with the basalts. For details regarding these quarries and their relation to the surrounding country, reference may be made to the Memoir on Sheet 32 (*Geology of Edinburgh and its Neighbourhood*, 1861, pp. 48 *et seq.*). It will be sufficient to notice here the general section at each opening, and the evidence of prolonged volcanic action in this part of the country.

27. At the north end of the east quarry of Kirkton, upon the upper

surface of a somewhat decomposing basalt, the following section may be observed :—

Black compact columnar basalt.

Green and black sandy shales, somewhat ashy in the upper part, containing well-preserved *Lepidodendrons, Stigmaria, Pecopteris*, &c.

Limestone, laminated fissile, with contorted laminæ, many of which have a finely mammillated or pisolitic surface.

(Covered space.)

Alternating thin bands of limestone and soft green calcareous volcanic tuff.

Limestone, varying rapidly in thickness (6 feet to 13 feet); hard, grey, with laminæ and lenticular nodules of chert; cavities sometimes lined with mammillary calcedony and crystallised calcite.

Thin bed, made of layers of similar limestone (full of volcanic dust and lapilli) and tuff.

Tuff, dirty green, concretionary, crumbling, seen at base of section and resting upon the next basalt-sheet.

This section clearly points to prolonged and energetic volcanic action at the locality. The basalts are true lava-flows, the tuffs represent the successive showers of volcanic dust and *debris;* while the limestones, as yet thoroughly barren of organic remains, appear to indicate the deposits of some geysers or thermal springs, the waters of which were charged, some with lime, some with silica, and filled a hollow on the hardened surface of a previous lava. That there was a forest or jungle at no great distance is shown by the number and excellent preservation of the terrestrial plants in the upper ashy shales. The uppermost basalt shows how the whole series of deposits, after doubtless a prolonged interval, was buried under a new outburst of lava.

28. The space between the two quarries appears to be occupied entirely by basalt; at least no other rock is visible, and the bottom of the road reveals everywhere projecting knobs of that rock. At the west quarry the following section was formerly observable, though, owing to the growth of the wood which has been planted there, the strata are not so well seen now.

Dark basalt (diabase).

Limestone, with thin layers of green tuff.

Limestone in thick beds; contains encrinites, corals, *productus*, &c.

Thin shale.

Green tuff.

Limestone, ashy and especially fossiliferous at the top, more shaly at the bottom.

Dirty-green, fine-grained, well-bedded tuff, containing a thin bed or vein of basalt 3 inches thick, and resting on a basalt-sheet.

This marine limestone, containing characteristic Carboniferous Limestone species of fossils, brings before us a great change from the conditions under which the strata of the east quarry were laid down. We see here evidence, that after the eruption of the lava which entombed the geyser basin, the area became sufficiently depressed to allow the sea to cover the site, while, though volcanic eruptions continued, as shown by the intercalations of tuff, the waters remained for long enough intervals sufficiently clear to permit the corals, crinoids, and other characteristic organisms of the sea of that time to flourish, and from their remains to form several beds of limestone. Reference was made in par. 16 to the occurrence of marine bands in the Calciferous Sandstone series, and even of beds of limestone containing typical Carboniferous Limestone fossils. Since there is neither stratigraphical nor palæontological break between these two divisions of the system any line of separation can only be drawn arbitrarily. It has been found convenient to take as the demarcation a very persistent band of limestone, known generally in the west of Scotland as the Hurlet Limestone. Sometimes this is the last of the encrinal limestones, and it then becomes a very evident and satisfactory boundary. Most frequently, however, one or more thin encrinal or *productus* limestones occur below it, containing similar fossils, but partly from their local development, and partly from their thinness, being less easily traceable. It is no doubt one of these lower bands which has been exposed in the west quarry of Kirkton. A few miles to the north a corresponding band occurs at Mid Tartraven (Sheet 32), but without the associated volcanic rocks so abundant southwards.

29. To the west of the Kirkton Quarries the ground is mainly covered by various basalt rocks in successive sheets, dipping westward at about 20°. Bands of tuff, sandstone, shale, or limestone, may occur in the longitudinal hollows between the outcrops of the basalts, but are not seen. The next visible stratum is the thick limestone of Petershill, which is regarded as the equivalent of the Hurlet Limestone, and as forming the base of the Carboniferous Limestone series. It is here from 70 to 80 feet thick, but this is quite an abnormal development, for it thins away rapidly both northward and southward. At Petershill it is overlaid by sandstones, shales, and ironstone of the usual character. It contains an abundant series of well-preserved fossils, and is seamed here and there with irregular layers and ragged flint-like nodules of chert. It can be followed northwards in a fine range of quarries for several miles as far as Hillhouse above Linlithgow (Sheet 32). In these openings an interesting opportunity is afforded of observing the rapid horizontal changes in the development of the volcanic rocks of the district. The overlying shales and sandstones continue to intervene between the limestone and the next succeeding sheet of basalt, but gradually diminish in thickness, until at the North Mine Quarry they are reduced to 20 feet, of which about half consists of layers of volcanic tuff. Four or five inches of coal occur almost immediately above the limestone here. At the same time a tuff, which is seen below the limestone at Galabraes, becomes thicker and more conspicuous towards the north.

30. Another limestone imbedded among the volcanic rocks occurs above the main or Petershill bed at Wardlaw. It is remarkable for the abundance of its corals, some layers of this rock consisting entirely of the close-set stems of *Lithostrotion irregulare*. It seems to die out to the north and south; at least it cannot be traced among the abundant volcanic masses of the district. The section at the old quarry of Wardlaw is as follows :—

Basalt, amygdaloidal and decomposing.
Dark sandy shale, with *calamites, producti*, &c.
Black pyritous shale, 3 or 4 inches.
Impure shaly limestone, about 2 feet.
Dark compact shale, 2 feet.
Limestone, 15 feet, including a band of *lithostrotion* at the bottom, and a similar band 10 to 15 inches thick at the top.
Light-greenish amygdaloidal basalt.

31. Above the Wardlaw Limestone comes a further pile of successive sheets of lava and tuff, forming the highest parts of the Bathgate and Linlithgow Hills. These igneous masses occupy the place of the greater part of the Borrowstounness and Bathgate coal-bearing series. Some of these upper coals, indeed, are found overlying the basalts at Hilderstone Hills and further north at Kipps; but between the latter point and Linlithgow no sections occur to show that any sedimentary beds are interstratified with the great sheets of volcanic material. A bore recently put down at the Mains Distillery went through successive beds of blue, green, and red "whin" (tuffs and decomposed basalt rocks), to the depth of 420.

feet, without meeting with any other kind of material. And probably the bore penetrated only the upper part of the series. A very saline water rose in the bore, possibly due to the liberation of some of the salt incrustations formed during the eruption of the volcanic rocks.[1] The first easily recognisable stratum overlying the thick volcanic series of these hills is the Index Limestone, so named from its serving as a guide to the position of the lower coals, all the more valuable of which lie beneath it. This seam may be seen overlying the sandstone at Hilderstone Quarry; it has also been met with at the surface close to the old coal-pit at Kipps. It is succeeded by still higher masses of basalt rocks, over which lie the two well-marked limestone bands, known locally as the Dykeneuk and Craigenbuck or Bowden seams. The former can be identified with the Calmy or Arden Limestone of Lanarkshire, the latter with the Castlecary or Levenseat band. Both seams are exposed in the ravine of the River Avon below Muiravonside. The upper is well seen also at the Bowden Lime-works. The Castlecary limestone is taken as the top of the Carboniferous Limestone series and base of the Mill-stone Grit.

32. (ii.) *Western Part of Borrowstounness Coal-field.*—To the north of the hills the volcanic masses rapidly diminish in thickness, while at the same time the normal strata of the Carboniferous Limestone series of the surrounding districts take their place. It will be observed from the Map that a considerable band, consisting partly of basalt and partly of tuffs, stretches northward beyond Liulithgow, as far as the shores of the Firth. This volcanic mass, measuring about 400 feet in thickness, divides the Borrowstounness coal-fields into two parts. (See Memoir of Sheet 32, p. 62 *et seq.*) Of the lower half, which contains most of the coals and the most valuable seam of ironstone, only a small patch lying to the north of Linlithgow Loch comes into the present Map. Owing, however, to the deep covering of drift in the valley between the hills to the south and those to the north of Linlithgow, it is impossible at present to draw any very satisfactory boundary lines for the respective limits of the igneous and the sedimentary rocks. The rocks of Bonnington Hill (Sheet 32) probably slant southwards under the thick deposit of sand, gravel, and clay, and join the main volcanic mass of the hills somewhere between the east end of Linlithgow and the Mains Distillery.

33. Of the portion of the Borrowstounness mineral field lying above the central volcanic zone, the following is the section :—

Craigenbuck or Castlecary Limestone, 7 or 8 feet.
    Strata—upwards of 300 feet.
Dykeneuk or Calmy Limestone, 7 feet.
    Strata—more than 400 feet.
Index Limestone, 2 feet 3 inches.
    Strata—including two or more sheets of basalt—140 feet.
Splint Coal, 2 feet 4 inches.
    Strata—100 to 120 feet.
Upper Ironstone (1 foot 5 inches) and 7 feet coal.
    Strata—60 to 70 feet.
Basalt-rocks.

The Upper Ironstone crops out at Borrowstounness about 120 feet west from the parish church, where it runs inland for about half a mile, beyond which, towards the south, it passes into coal and shale. The Splint Coal has been worked from the sea for more than a mile inland. Southwards, however, considerable disturbance appears to have taken place, so that though coal seams have been found and worked, it is not always easy to parallel them with those of which the position is known in the more

[1] It contained 140 grs. of sodium chloride per gallon. See *Proc. Roy. Soc. Edin.* vol. ix. p. 367.

regular part of the Borrowstounness field. Between the Splint Coal and the Index Limestone a bed of basalt, about 50 feet thick, occurs at the Snab Pit. Either a diminished prolongation of this bed or a higher band occurs in a section at Kinneil Distillery. It is almost immediately covered by the Index Limestone, which is here 2 feet 3 inches thick, and contains abundance of the small variety of *Productus giganteus*, crinoids, &c. From want of sections of this seam, so useful as a horizon in tracing the structure of the coal-fields, cannot be followed inland. There appears to be some confusion in that direction, arising partly perhaps from a thinning away of some portion of the ordinary stratified rocks and the consequent approach of the volcanic sheets of Bonnytoun Hill, towards the line of the higher limestones on the River Avon. There seems likewise to be some dislocation of the rocks about the position of the white line on the Map to the south of Swordie Mains.

34. The strata overlying the Index Limestone have been quarried extensively to the east of Kinneil Iron-Works. First comes a bed of fireclay, about $3\frac{1}{2}$ feet thick, largely used for making bricks, &c. This is followed by a zone of coarse yellow sandstone, 79 feet thick. A seam of coal, about 2 feet thick, with a thin shale parting, lies about $14\frac{1}{2}$ feet above this sandstone in the Snab Pit section. This is probably the seam known as the Mount Hunger coal, which had formerly been worked to some extent inland from Borrowstounness. Above this seam we enter upon a thick series of sandstones and shales, with a few poor thin seams of coal. A band of " whinstone," like that below the Index Limestone, occurs on the coast at Snab, and runs inland by the Snab Pit. Another much thinner band crops on the beach, 150 yards to the south-west of Snab Cottage.

35. The limestone of Dykeneuk may be identified with the Calmy, Gair, Janet Peat or Arden Limestone of other parts of the great Scottish coal-fields. It consists of three seams, separated by shale (or "blaes"), as under:—

	Feet.	Inches.
Dark blue blaes, ...	19	0
Limestone, ...	1	8
Blue blaes, ...	1	11
Limestone, . . .	1	8
Soft blaes, ...	0	7
Limestone, ...	1	0
Blue fireclay and blaes, . .	3	11

The seam, dipping gently westward, runs inland under the deep cover of boulder-clay, but has been laid bare by the River Avon above Kinneil Mills and at Little Mill, as well as in the course of a small brook which falls into the river from the north side between these two places. It appears to have thinned out considerably in this part of its course. Possibly its formation may have been affected here by a thick zone of green tuff, which lies almost immediately below it. It recrosses the channel of the Avon about 200 yards below Linlithgow Bridge, but keeps parallel with the river, and is again exposed in the cliffs below Woodcockdale House. It has now recovered its usual triple division and thickness. It is last seen in the wooded bank below Easter Carriber. From that point the crop strikes south-eastward into Linlithgowshire. Unless it disappears it must lie between some of the great parallel volcanic bands; but its course has not been made out. We do not again meet with it as a traceable band in the rest of the eastern part of the Map, though it has been met with in several bores to the south of Bathgate.

36. After an interval of more than 300 feet of strata, consisting of shales and sandstones with no important or marked seam of any kind, the uppermost limestone occurs. This may be confidently identified with the well known Castlecary or Levenseat Limestone. It begins on the

coast at Craigenbuck, where it is seen overlying the yellow sandstone which has there been quarried. The best section of it, however, is that in the cliff of the Avon close to the viaduct of the Slamannan and Borrowstounness Railway. The following table shows the arrangement of the strata at that place :—

	Feet.	Inches
Blue shale, ...	3	9
Coarse clay ironstone, . .	1	4
Hard blue shale, . . .	1	4
Rib of hard shaly limestone, . .	0	6
Soft bluish shale, . . .	8	0
Limestone, grey crystalline, . : .	4	4
Shale parting, ...	0	6
Limestone, concretionary, . . .	0	10
Limestone, concretionary, . . .	0	3
Limestone, compact blue, . .	1	1
Shale, blue and pale grey, . .	6	0
Shaly sandstone and dark shale, .	4	0

With the exception of the thin parting of shale, it forms one bed between 6 and 7 feet in thickness. Following the same course as the Calmy seam below, it strikes into Stirlingshire, but again crosses the Avon at the canal aqueduct and below the house of Muiravonside. As already mentioned (par. 31), it has been extensively quarried under the basalt mass of Bowden Hill.

37. (iii.) *The Area to the South of Bathgate.*—Partly owing to the thick covering of drift, and partly to the want of natural sections, little is seen of the limestone series between Bathgate and the southern edge of the Map. The Main or Hurlet Limestone first appears near Red House, about two miles and a half to the south-east of Bathgate, where it has been quarried to a small extent, and where its underlying coal-seam has a thickness of between 4 and 5 feet. It crops also in the channel of the River Almond a quarter of a mile below Blackburn. In the section cut by that stream there likewise appears, about 300 feet further east, a lower and much thinner encrinal limestone, lying among grey shales. Two higher limestones may be seen in the same section. One of these, about 8 feet thick, crosses the river about 600 feet west from the Hurlet Limestone. It must lie about 250 feet above that limestone, with an intervening mass of shaly sandstones and shales. The highest calcareous band seen in the Avon section is a limestone about $1\frac{1}{2}$ or 2 feet thick, with a seam of coal (8 or 9 inches) lying below it. It occurs immediately to the east of Blackburn, under the remarkable rock which is quarried as "lakestone " (par. 39). But probably still another limestone band crops a little further west above Blackburn Bridge, at least, if no fault intervenes, such a band, which is proved by borings to crop at Murrayfield, should cross the river there. These limestones no doubt represent the Hosie's group.

38. The Hurlet Limestone is next visible in the Breich Water at Addiewell. It is there associated with its accompanying strata as follows :— The limestone can be followed southwards partly by quarries on its crop, and partly by pits which have been sunk to the Hurlet coal. It crosses the Longhill Burn near the White Sykes, and then bends south-eastward into Sheet 31. The Breich Water affords a good section of the immediately overlying beds. A 3 feet coal-seam crops about 650 feet above Addiewell Bridge. A higher limestone (one of the Hosie's bands) crosses where the Skolie Burn joins the Breich Water, and is well exposed in the channel of the lower part of the former stream. With it are associated some shales and a thin limestone band charged with fossils (see Appendix). What may be the same limestone is found close to the shooting-lodge on the small stream which descends to the east from Hendrey's

Course. Above the position of this limestone a seam of blind coal, 14 inches thick, is said to crop at Kirkhill. The Longford main coal (3 feet thick), the chief seam in the district, crosses the Breich Water about a quarter of a mile above the mouth of the Skolie Burn. Its outcrop strikes southward.

39. In the lower limestone group of the area now described we observe the most southerly prolongations of the thick volcanic masses of the Bathgate and Linlithgow Hills. Owing to the obscured nature of the surface immediately to the south of Bathgate, hardly any solid rock can be seen. But the ground has been extensively bored for minerals, with the result of showing that one or two bands of the lavas from the north run southward to about the neighbourhood of Blackburn. One of these forms the "lakestone" already referred to in par. 37, which has been largely used as a good material for the soles of ovens. A somewhat similar rock runs from the Breich Water southwards for two miles. This rock, as quarried near Blackburn, consists of two beds, or at least of an upper and under portion, only the latter of which is used for oven-soles. This part is a serpentinous rock, dull greenish-black in colour, speckled with crystals of augite and olivine, soapy to the touch, and traversed with threads of chrysotile. Under the microscope it is seen to consist of a serpentinous ground-mass, through which are dispersed numerous crystals of olivine almost entirely serpentinized, well preserved crystals of augite, abundant prisms of apatite, with some titaniferous iron; occasional scales of biotite, and minute prisms of a brown strongly dichroic mineral, which may be hornblende. The rock seems to have been originally an augitic-olivine rock, and to approach most closely to Gümbel's palæopikrite. It is the only example of such a rock at present known to occur in central Scotland. The upper part, or bed of the rock, resembles some of the altered basalts or diabases of the district. It consists of abundant triclinic felspar and augite, both in small prisms, large crystals of olivine altered into serpentine, a little titaniferous iron or magnetite, and a little apatite. There is a little glassy ground-mass.

40. The three limestone bands of the uppermost group of the Carboniferous Limestone series have not been traced continuously south from Bathgate, owing partly to the depth of drift, and partly to the scantiness of borings and other trials for minerals. That they do reach beyond Bathgate is shown by the fact that they have all three been found in bores to the east of Durhamtown. A limestone, perhaps the Index seam, has been cut in some borings to the north of Burnbrae.

41. The highest, or the Levenseat Limestone, however, appears in force towards the southern margin of the Map, where a part of the Wilsontown field is shown, a description of which has been given in the Memoir explanatory of Sheet 23. It is well seen at Levenseat (whence its local name), the section there being as follows :—

	Inches.
Boulder-clay,	
Sandstone debris and blocks,	
Sandstone with faikes, and sandy and shaly partings,	
Grey fireclay,	4 to 6
Black shale,	3 to 4
Daugh, or dark dirty shaly fireclay,	2 to 4
Black oil-shale,	5 to 7
Shaly fireclay parting,	1 to 3
Limestone,	9 feet.
Shale,	

Another limestone has formerly been worked, but to a small extent, a little to the east of Levenseat, near Whitehouse. This appears to be the same seam as the Gair limestone of Carluke (see Memoir explanatory of Sheet 23).

b. THE DENNY DISTRICT.

42. Under this division is included that portion of the Carboniferous Limestone area which runs from the northern edge of the Map southwards to the Banknock and Dennyloanhead coal-field. Its western boundary is formed by the volcanic masses of the Kilsyth Fells, on the south it is truncated by a large fault, on the east it dips below the Millstone Grit. The annexed table gives the nature and order of the chief strata composing the Limestone series of this district.

Vertical Section of the Carboniferous Limestone Series in the Denny District.

Group		Approximate thickness.		
		Fms.	Ft.	In.
	Castlecary Limestone, ...	0	7	0
	Strata—chiefly thin bedded, including a thin band of limestone and several clay ironstones, . . .	10	0	0
	Strata—details unknown, contain some thick sandstones, probably . .	70–80	0	0
	Limestone, 1 foot) Blaes, 6 in. } Calmy Limestone, . Limestone, 2 feet)	0	3	6
Upper Group.	Strata, ...	8	0	0
	Hirst Coal, ...	0	1	5
	Strata, ...	1	3	0
	Low Hirst Coal, ...	0	0	2-3
	Strata—including a thin coal or so, and a thick sandstone from 6 to 16 fms., .	23–33	0	0
	Limestone (sometimes awanting), .	0	1	3
	Strata,—including a very thick grit or sandstone, and a thin variable coal-seam or two, ...	20–30	0	0
	Index Limestone, ...	0	4	0
	Strata, ...	8	0	0
	Coal, 8 in.) Parting, 7 in. } Garth Coal, . . Coal 1 foot,)	0	2m	2-3
	Strata, ...	23–25	0	0
	Parrot coal, 2 in. . Denny Black Black-band ironst., 1 foot 3 in. band Iron- Daugh, 1 in. . . stone (Poasil Parrot coal, 4 in. . position, .	0	1	10
	Strata, ...	20	0	0
	Coal, Bannockburn main, 1 ft. 5 in. to .	0	3	0
	Strata, ...	13	0	0
Middle Group.	Clay-band ironstone, . . .	0	1	0
	Strata, ...	0	3	3
	Clay-band ironstone, . . .	0	0	6¼
	Strata, ...	11	0	0
	Clay-band ironstone, . . .	0	0	6½
	Strata, ...	3	0	0
	Coal, . . .	0	0	3
	Strata, . . .	0	4	0
	Limestone, . . .	0	0	8
	Strata, . . .	12	0	0
	Foul coal, . . .	0	0	5
	Strata, . . .	9	0	0
	Coal, . . .	0	0	4
	Strata, . . .	10	0	0
	Foul coal, . . .	0	0	8
	Strata, . . .			
Lower Group.	Hosie's Limestones, . . . Strata, . . .			

Hurlet Limestone (burnt and altered by intrusive rocks at Denny).

43. The Hurlet Limestone is the lowest recognisable bed in the series, all below that horizon being concealed by a great intrusive sheet of basalt, which, though now much interrupted by faults, once extended continuously from Coney Park, at least as far north as the Abbey Craig at Stirling (Sheet 39). The limestone is seen in the bed of the Carron Water, lying above the basalt rock and much altered. A few yards to the north it is cut out entirely by that rock, and the sandstone in connection with it is altered into a hard quartz-rock. The "Hosie's" seams are represented by a few thin bands seen in the Carron, where they occur among sandstones and shales with a few thin nodular bands of clay ironstone. To the north, and just about the edge of the present Map, they are much thicker, and have been largely quarried at Northfield and Quarter.

44. The middle group shows a considerable difference from the arrangement that obtains in the Kilsyth district immediately to the west (see par. 46). Only two seams of black-band ironstone occur : they lie about the horizon of the three upper ones at Kilsyth, but it is not easy to determine which of these three seams they represent, as the latter are dying out northwards. No. 4, or the Banton Ironstone, so important in the Kilsyth field, is either not present or not recognisable. None of the coal-seams of Kilsyth are workable at Denny, and many have either died out altogether, or are represented by beds only a few inches in thickness. The only seam at present worked is the Bannockburn Main Coal, which occupies the position of one of the Highland Park seams of Kilsyth. Denny thus seems to occupy an intermediate place between Kilsyth on the one hand and Bannockburn on the other, the beds of both fields being thin where they overlap or dovetail. Near Low Quarter numerous clay-band ironstones are seen in the burn, and have been wrought by the Carron Iron Company. They probably represent some of the Banton clay-bands. The southern extension of the Bannockburn coal-field enters the present Sheet for a short distance until cut off by a large fault. It will be treated of in the Explanation to Sheet 39.

45. The Index Limestone, which forms the base of the highest group, is persistent through the field, and taken in conjunction with a massive sandstone or grit which underlies it, forms an unmistakable horizon for those in search of the lower seams. The Calmy or Arden Limestone is accompanied by its two coal-seams, the Upper Hirst and Lower Hirst, as at Kilsyth and in the Bannockburn field. The Castlecary Limestone, where exposed at Doghillock, presents much the same characters as at Castlecary. North of that point, however, it splits up into several seams, each separated from the other by a considerable thickness of intervening strata. The higher part of this group consists greatly of sandstones, which appear to be swelling out northwards. At the edge of the present Map, and in Sheet 39, they are extensively quarried. Except as regards the presence of the limestone, the conditions of deposit seem to have been very much like those which produced the overlying Millstone Grit.

c. Cumbernauld and Kilsyth District.

46. This district embraces the Carboniferous Limestone area lying between Kirkintilloch and the Denny district. It is bounded on the north by the large faults which separate it from the older rocks of the Kilsyth Fells ; on the south by the long fault and basalt dyke, which cut the Stirlingshire coal-field ; on the east by the Millstone Grit under which it dips ; while on the west it is separated by no proper line from the Lennoxtown district, into which it merges. The succession of the beds is shown in the following table. In preparing this table details were obtained

from borings, &c., of the strata from the Castlecary Limestone to the lower Hirst coal. From that point down to within twenty-three fathoms of the Index Limestone, where no such information was obtainable, the nature and thickness of the beds has been made out from the study of their outcrops. Below this interval details are given from mining operations as far as the Kilsyth Main Coal. The section has been continued downward to show the relative positions of the Limestones of the lower group, though no bores were procured to illustrate the nature of the intervening strata.

Vertical Table of the Carboniferous Limestone Series in the Cumbernauld and Kilsyth District.

		Approximate thickness.		
		Fms.	Ft.	In.
Upper.	Castlecary Limestone, in three beds with partings, ...	0	7	0
	Strata—including some thick sandstones and thin coals, ...	70–80	0	0
	Strata—consisting chiefly of dark blaes and ironstone and limestone nodules, . .	4–10	0	0
	Calmy or Arden Limestone, in three beds with blue shale partings, ...	0	7	6
	Strata, ...	1	2	0
	Coal, "Upper Hirst,"	0	3	9
	Strata, ...	2	4	0
	Coal "Lower Hirst,"	0	1	6½
	Strata—including some thick coarse friable grits, say	40–50	0	0
	Free coal, ...	0	0	5
	Strata, ...	3	0	0
	Foul coal, ...	0	1	0
	Strata, . . .	0	3	8
	Free coal, . . .	0	0	3
	Strata, . .	3	0	0
	Foul coal, . .	0	1	8
	Strata, . .	17	0	0
	Index Limestone, . . .	0	3	10
Middle.	Intrusive Basalt (the position of this is variable), Strata, . . .	8	0	0
	Coal with parting, . . .	0	1	8
	Strata, . . .	3	0	0
	Coal, . . .	0	0	9
	Strata, . . .	5	0	0
	No. 1 Ironstone, Black-band (coal, ironstone, and partings), . . .	0	1	2
	Strata, . . .	6	0	0
	Foul coal, . . .	0	0	6
	Strata, . . .	6	0	0
	Foul coal, . . .	0	1	9
	Strata, . . .	4	0	0
	Coal, "Gartshore." . . .	0	4	0
	Strata, . . .	5	0	0
	No. 2 Ironstone, Black-band (Craw coal and ironstone), "Gartshore Upper Ironstone;" .	0	0	8
	Strata, . . .	1	0	0
	Foul coal, . . .	0	1	9
	Strata, . . .	3	0	0
	No. 3 Ironstone, Black-band (coal and ironstone), "Neilston," . . .	0	1	6
	Strata—including three clay-band ironstones of an aggregate thickness of 4½ inches, .	2	0	0
	Coal, . . .	0	2	3
	Strata, . . .	9	0	0
	Smithy coal, {Highland Park seams.	0	2	0
	Strata, Position of Bannockburn	8	0	0
	Coal, "Neilston,' and Denny seams . . }	0	3	10

	Approximate thickness.		
	Fms.	Ft.	In.
Strata—Position of Banton clay-band iron-stones,	1	0	0
No. 4 Ironstone, "Banton black-band,"	0	1	2
Strata,	7	0	0
Coal, "Banton Upper Smithy,"	0	1	10
Strata,	8	0	0
Coal, Kilsyth caking or main, "Banton Main,"	0	4	0
Strata,			
Banton Smithy Coal,			
Strata,			
Hosie's Limestones, in two or three thin bands, separated by various thicknesses of strata. One of the intermediate masses is a thick zone of blue shales, with numerous bands of clay-ironstone,			
Strata,			
Hurlet Limestone,			
Strata,			
Limestone,			

Rows bracketed on the left: **Middle** (from first row through Strata below Banton Smithy Coal); **Lower** (Hosie's Limestones through Limestone).

47. The dip of the rocks being on the whole towards the east, the lowest portions of this limestone series are met with in the western parts of the district. It will be seen from the Map how much these western and northern tracts have been broken by faults, invaded by intrusive igneous rocks, and formed into small basins. The lowest of the three limestone groups is only exposed here in three different places, where its strata peep out against the large fault which flanks the Campsie Hills. These are most typically seen in the Corrie and Queenzie Burns, and their tributaries between the two parallel faults. There, immediately overlying the tuffs of the Cement-stone group, a thin white concretionary limestone occurs full of encrinite-stems and corals. A few fathoms higher a thick bed of blue limestone has been extensively quarried. It represents the Hurlet Limestone. Not more than ten feet of alternating beds of lime-stone and shale are visible, the base being never exposed. For at least fifty fathoms in ascending order, the succeeding strata consist more or less of blue clay-shales, with nodules and bands of clay ironstone, with at least three thin bands of limestone known as the "Hosie's." One of the above-mentioned burns exposes a cliff of from 80 to 100 feet of these blue clays, with layer above layer of clay ironstone nodules. Towards the upper limit of the Hosie's Limestone, the intervening strata contain several beds of sandstone. One band of sandy shale is crowded with a *Lingula*. Two of the Hosie's bands were formerly wrought near Banton, and burnt into a hydraulic cement. Near Banton the Hurlet Limestone is scarcely recognisable even as a limestone, for at the only place where it is exposed, in a small burn which enters the Banton coal-field, it is greatly altered by contact with a basalt dyke.

48. A marked characteristic of the strata of this district is their richness in the economic minerals belonging to the middle group of the Lime-stone series—more especially in Black-band ironstone—four different seams of which are wrought in the district. Those numbered from 1 to 3 occupy the horizon of the well-known Possil bands. They are very variable in thickness and quality, even in the same coal-field. For instance, No. 1 dies out to the west, and number 2 becomes the upper ironstone at Gartshore. No. 4, or Banton Black-band ironstone, is also local, though where found it is of remarkably good quality. The clay-band ironstones are even more variable, for in the Banton part of the district there occurs a horizon of several fathoms of shales, with at least

ten or eleven bands of clay ironstone, which were formerly wrought by the Carron Iron Company and made into excellent iron. Some of the bands were at least one foot thick, and exhibited cone in cone structure. In the neighbourhood of Kilsyth these have either entirely disappeared, or are only represented by one or two intermittent bands. The coals seem to behave very much in the same manner; a seam which is workable at one end of the field being often found thin and worthless at the other. Almost every colliery has a seam called after itself, and which is seldom workable anywhere else. The Banton Main, or Kilsyth Caking Coal, is the most persistent, as well as the best and most sought after. From its caking nature it is considered almost as good as the best Newcastle coal, and commands a ready sale in Glasgow as a house coal, whither there is an easy carriage by canal. The dross makes a good coke for foundries, &c. In connection with the variable nature of the coal-seams of the district, it may be as well to mention that the coals which occur between Nos. 3 and 4 ironstones were formerly wrought near Kilsyth, under the name of "Highland Park" seams. Even there they were thin; but at Banton they are only a few inches thick each. At Denny and Bannockburn (Sheet 30) they swell out, and form the workable seams of those districts.

49. The members of the upper group of the Limestone series make up a considerable part of the surface of the district. The lowest bed is the Index Limestone, which, though thin, is of good quality, and was quarried formerly at Dullatur, on the railway, about midway between Castlecary and Croy. It is of more value, however, as a horizon or "position" than as a source of lime, lying as it does just above the economic minerals of the middle group. About 70 to 80 fathoms above it comes the Calmy or Arden Limestone. It is made up of three thin layers, separated by partings of blue shale. It is not now quarried here, though, to judge from the number of openings along its outcrop, it must have been extensively wrought in former times. The chief interest of this band now is that it has two coal-seams associated with it, at a depth of a few fathoms beneath it, which are much sought after in the neighbourhood of Cumbernauld. They are known as the Hirst Coals. The upper one is the thicker; but the under one, having the quality, so rare in Scotland, of caking, is considered the better. The strata above the Calmy Limestone are thin to the south of the district, and thicken out rapidly northward. The uppermost bed is a limestone known as the "Castlecary Limestone," from its being extensively mined there. It too is thin at the southern margin of the area, being not above 18 inches to 2 feet thick. At Castlecary, where it consists of three beds of different quality, separated by shaly partings, the aggregate thickness of the limestone bands amounts to 7 feet. It makes an excellent lime when burnt, and is also good as a flux for iron-making, for which purpose it was employed by the Carron Iron Company.

d. Lennoxtown and Cadder District.

50. A portion of the Campsie mineral field comes into the area of the present Map, with Lennoxtown as its centre. It will be seen that the large fault bounding the southern edge of the Campsie Fells forms the northern limit of this limestone district, the Hurlet coal and limestone, with the Hosie's and overlying seams, being abruptly truncated against the base of the steep slopes. From that sharply defined boundary-line southward by Lennoxtown, the strata lie as a flat cake, which has been trenched in many places by descending water-courses, and has been hollowed out into the valley of the Glazert. So gentle is the inclination that the coals and other seams have been worked from side to side of the

south hill of Campsie, which is thus undermined in all directions. The sinuous outcrops upon the Map are consequently the result of the irregular denudation of the district, rather than of any marked change in angle or direction of dip of the rocks. It will be observed, too, that numerous dislocations have broken up this outcrop into many detached portions. A section, drawn from the base of the hills above Lennoxtown due south to the Kelvin, shows the Hurlet Limestone lying against the older porphyrites, followed underneath by its well-known coal-seam, and then by the White Limestone and other lower strata down to the massive white quartzose sandstone of Craigend Moor, which forms the floor of the valley. The same series of strata rises bed above bed on the southern side of the Glazert, passes under the South Hill, and reappears on the southern slopes of that ridge which repeats the section at Lennoxtown. But a large fault now interferes; the whole of the lower limestone groups are thrown down to the south, and, after a space of less than a mile, the uppermost or Calmy Limestone appears overlaid by the Millstone Grit.

51. It is thus particularly the lower portions of the Carboniferous Limestone series which are developed in this district. The following table represents the general order of succession among the beds :—

Section of Strata near Lennoxtown.

	Fms.	Ft.	In.
Shales and ironstone bands, ...	14	3	9
Hosie or black limestone, ...	1	0	0
Shale, with four bands of clay ironstone, . .	1	0	0
Blue shales with partings and nodules of clay ironstone,	22	2	0
Hurlet (Campsie Main) limestone, . .	0	4	0
Alum shale, ...	0	2	0
Hurlet or Main coal, ...	0	3	8
Under clay, ...	0	0	7
White (entomostracan) limestone, . .	0	4	6
Hard flinty sandstone ("Kingle"), . .	0	4	6
Shale, ...	1	1	4
Limestone (encrinal), ...	0	0	10
Sandy shale ("Fakes"), . . .	0	0	10
Alum shale, ...	0	0	9
Parrot coal, ...	0	0	4
Common coal, ...	0	0	10
Fireclay, ...	1	2	6

52. The sections in some of the water-courses which have been cut into the south hill show the existence in the district of a number of thin encrinal limestones, with associated shales and thin coals below the horizon of the Hurlet Limestone.[1] Below these marine strata lie the massive white sandstones and conglomerates of Craigmaddie Moor, among and below which many other thin limestones and shales have been met with in boring. All these rocks, however, are later in date than the volcanic sheets of the Campsie Hills, on which they may be seen distinctly to rest at the west end of Craigmaddie Moor.

53. The limestones have been opened in many quarries, though these are now in large measure disused. The alum shale has long been extensively worked. It sometimes reaches a thickness of 14 feet, but only the lower pyritous portion near the coal is profitably extracted. The presence of so much sulphide of iron destroys the value of the Main coal. That seam was formerly extensively worked in this district, but is now superseded by better coal brought from other coal-fields by railway. The

[1] See a paper on the Campsie District, by J. Young, *Trans. Geol. Soc. Glasgow*, vol. i.

nodular clay-band ironstones, below the Hosie's Limestone, were also at one time mined to a considerable extent; but the workings have long been abandoned.

54. South of the tongue of Millstone Grit, which runs down the valley of the Kelvin, the upper limestone group occupies a sinuous band along the edge of the Map, as far as the great fault which runs in an east and west direction through Hogganfield Loch. The uppermost or Castlecary Limestone has not yet been identified in that quarter, so that the Calmy or Robroyston Limestone, with its associated coal, is taken here as the top of the Carboniferous Limestone series.

Millstone Grit.

55. This formation consists here of a group of grey, white, yellow, and sometimes red coarse-grained sandstones, shales, fireclays, thin beds of more or less impure limestones, and some seams of coal. It is known locally as the " Moorstone rock," from the fact that the ground which it underlies forms tracks of bare moor, with protruding knobs of the harder sandstones or grits, except where, as in the low country near the Forth, a superficial covering of boulder-clay or other drift obscures the strata below. Everywhere within the area of the present Map this sandy series intervenes between the Carboniferous Limestone series below and the Coal-measures above. Nevertheless, its position on the surface is not that of a continuous and nearly equal band. Owing partly to changes in the angle and direction of the dip, partly to unequal denudation, and partly to the effects of many transverse faults, the strip of Millstone Grit has acquired a broken sinuous course. It is most regular on the east side of the great Coal-measure basin, being there continuously traceable across the Map, in a north and south direction from the Firth of Forth into Lanarkshire. For a short space north of Falkirk, cutting across the Coal-measure triangle which it thus divides into two, it joins the western band. On that side of the basin its course, as shown on the Map, becomes exceedingly irregular. A tolerably uniform belt of the Millstone Grit runs indeed from Torwood southward to the great basalt dyke and fault at the southern end of Fannyside Moor. But by that dislocation it is cut completely across and shifted westwards, the Carboniferous Limestone series and Coal-measures being for nearly two miles brought directly against each other. From this point the band turns to the west as far as the line of the Robroyston Limestone between Millerston and Kirkintilloch, but sends a long tongue northwards and eastwards up the vale of the Kelvin. There are thus three well-marked tracts of Millstone Grit in the present district.

56. The eastern tract from the Gladsmuir Hills to the Forth forms a belt about eighteen miles long, averaging rather more than a mile in breadth. The only minerals worked in this band are a seam of clay-ironstone nodules, known as "Thomson's Balls," or "The Ginstone," which were formerly mined near the village of Greenburgh, in the valley of the Breich Water; and the Curly or Curdly ironstone. This last-named seam is a clay ironstone of irregular thickness, which occurs lower down in the series. It has been worked in the moory tracts that lie between the outcrop of the Levenseat limestone and Muldron. There are about 30 fathoms of strata between the Ginstone and the Curly ironstone.

57. The north-western tract, including all the areas that appear to the north and north-west of the Coal-measures, is notable for the excellence of its fireclays. These are worked chiefly at Garnkirk, Gartcosh, Glenboig, and Gartverry. Several beds are worked as under :—

	Fms.	Ft.	Iu.
Garnkirk upper working, ...	1	1	7
Strata, ...	7	3	0
Garnkirk under or Heathfield upper working,	1	5	1
Strata, ...	27	0	0
Gartcosh upper working, ...	0	3	3
Strata, ...	3	0	0
Glenboig upper working, . .	1	2	10
Strata, ...	6	3	0
Gartcosh middle or Glenboig lower working,	0	1	8
Strata, ...	22	3	0
Gartcosh lower working, ...	0	4	2
Strata, . . .	2 to 5	0	0
Carboniferous limestone series.			

As already stated (par. 54), the base of the Millstone Grit in this portion of the Map is not marked by the same limestone as in the central and eastern parts of the district. The highest (Castlecary or Levenseat) limestone has not been traced in this western area, where consequently it has been necessary to take the next seam below it (the Robroyston or Calmy).

58. In the northern tract, or that which forms the western boundary of the Falkirk coal-field, the strata consist as usual mainly of thick coarse sandstones, with partings of shale and fireclay, and occasionally of coal-seams and clay-ironstones. Of the ironstones one seam is so calcareous that it can be used as a cement, and is known as the "Roman Cement." A curious bed of ironstone seems to have been wrought on Fannyside Moor, at the west end of the lochs. Fragments of a brown pisolitic and concretionary ironstone are there found among rubbish heaps. This would seem to be an extension northwards of the Curly or Curdly band ironstone alluded to in par. 56. To judge from the "smuts," a coal-seam must also have been formerly wrought in this series near Abronhill. In no part of the district contained within the Map can the characteristic features of the Millstone Grit, or "Moorstone Rock," be better seen than in the range of high ground stretching north from Fannyside Moor to near Bonnybridge, and again in the uplands of Torwood. On this side of the coal-field it seems to be thickening out towards the north, for on the farm of Drum, four miles S.W. from Falkirk, the distance from the slaty-band ironstone (the base of the coal-measures) to the Castlecary Limestone is about 90 fathoms, while to the north of Larbert the distance between these two seams is much greater.

Coal-Measures.

59. The Coal-measures occupy rather more than half the area of the Map, and form, strictly speaking, merely a continuation of the great Clyde basin (see Sheet 23). Examined in detail, this northern prolongation of the Clyde basin is found to consist of a number of subsidiary basins. Thus we have first, the Clyde basin proper, the deepest portion of which is in the valley of the Clyde near Uddingston. It is bounded on the north by the large fault that runs east from Hogganfield Loch to New Monkland; and on the east by the broken anticlinal axis that strikes north from the South Calder near Murdoston, by Goodockhill, Clarkston, and Rawyards, until it meets the large fault near New Monkland. The basins lying north and east of this are neither so deep nor so well defined, owing to rapid undulations of the strata, which bring up the same beds again and again to the surface. This is well shown in the moory tract between Stand and Binniehill, where several broken and interrupted basins appear, which, however, form in reality only one main basin,

whereof the deepest part lies near Arden. The connection of this basin with the coal-fields of Shotts, Fauldhouse, and Torbanehill is obscured by great intrusions of basalt, and probably also by dislocations. Disregarding minor undulations, however, it is still possible to trace the outline of one main basin which includes all the coal-fields just mentioned. The lip of this basin is formed in the west by the broken anticlinal axis which separates it from the coal-fields of the Clyde. Followed southwards, the strike gradually swings round to the east, the beds rising up so as to dip northwards at Stane. Thereafter, the eastern margin of the Coal-measures forms the edge of the basin as far as the basalt dyke. This dyke, which is also a line of dislocation throughout the greater part of its course, coincides (near Slamannan) with another anticlinal axis that forms the northern boundary of the basin. The deepest part of this composite and irregular basin lies, as before-mentioned, in the moory ground near Arden, from which point the beds flatten out with many undulations towards the east and south-east.

60. North of the long basalt dyke between Slamannan and Falkirk we find another basin, which, if of less extent than the one just described, is better defined. Part of a fourth basin is seen at Carron. It is separated from that of Falkirk and Slamannan by a ridge of Millstone Grit, and forms a portion of the Stirling and Alloa coal-fields. The only other basin shown upon the Map is the small isolated one near Denny-loanhead.

61. The Coal-measures consist of two groups: First, an upper set of reddish sandstones, arenaceous shales, fireclays, and sandy marls, with now and again a thin seam of coal; and, second, a lower group of white and grey sandstones, flags, dark bluish-grey and black shales, fireclays, and numerous seams of coal, as well as black-band and clay-band iron-stones. The upper group probably rests unconformably upon the lower group, but the unconformability is so gentle that it might readily escape notice in this part of the coal-field area of Scotland. It is better marked in the region embraced by Sheet 23, and still more decidedly in the coal-fields of Ayrshire. The coal-fields in the present Map will be arranged for convenient description nearly as in the separate basins mentioned above, namely—1. The Clyde basin; 2. the North-central basin, embracing the mineral fields of Arden, Stand, Greengairs, Binniehill, Armadale, Grangemouth, Carron, Torbanehill, Fauldhouse, Bowhousebog, Shotts, and Benhar; 3. the Falkirk and Slamannan coal-fields; 4. the Coneybank and Banknock basins.

1. The Clyde Basin.

62. This basin includes the coal-fields of Cambuslang, Tollcross, Shettleston, Baillieston, Coatbridge, Airdrie, Calderbank and Chapelhall, Holytown, Newarthill, Cleland, &c., and those in the centre of the basin around Uddingston. Full descriptions and details of these coal-fields will be given in the extended Memoir; all that can be done here is to show the general succession of the seams that occur within the limits of this basin, and the others that fall to be described in this Memoir. It is in the neighbourhood of the River Clyde that the Coal-measures attain their greatest thickness—the Upper Red Sandstone series coming on in considerable force, so as to cover a wide area in the centre of the basin. These beds are represented on the Map by the darker shade, and it will be observed that owing to powerful faults they reappear to the north of the principal or central area, forming a broad belt or band that stretches from the east end of Glasgow, past Baillieston and Old Monkland, to

Woodhall. The distance between the base of the red beds and the upper-most coal-seam is variable, reaching from a few fathoms up to 40 or 50 fathoms.

63. The following table gives the names of the various seams of coal and ironstone which occur within the area of the Clyde basin, so far as that is represented upon this Map. The thicknesses given are averages. This table should be compared with that which is given in the Explanatory Memoir to accompany Sheet 23, at p. 36.

Red Sandstones, &c.

	Fms.	Ft.	In.
Palacecraig Ironstone; a blackband of local occurrence at Palace-craig and Faskine, North Calder Water,	0	0	9
Strata,	16	0	0
Upper Coal; worked chiefly near Glasgow, where it attains 5 ft. in thickness. In the southern and eastern part of the basin it is thin, generally of poor quality, and unworkable,	0	5	0
Strata from 16 fms. to 20 fms.,	17	2	0
Ell Coal; extensively worked; varies in thickness from 2 ft. 2 in. to 10 ft. Now and again it is divided by partings into two, three, and sometimes four seams. In some parts of the basin it is considered unworkable,	0	5	6
Strata from 6 fms to 8 fms.,	6	2	0
Pyotshaw Coal; extensively worked; varies in thickness from 3 ft. to 6 ft.,	0	4	0
Strata, from a mere parting of an inch or so up to 8 fms.,	3	3	0
Main Coal; extensively worked; varies in thickness from 2 ft. to 5 ft. 6 in.,	0	4	2
[The Pyotshaw and Main coals frequently come together, so as to form one seam, with an average thickness of 4 ft. or 5 ft. Occasionally the Main coal is separated into two seams by the intercalation of a parting from a few inches to a foot or more in thickness.]			
Strata, from 8 fms. to 10 fms.,	9	0	0
Humph Coal; very little worked; wanting in some places; varies from 2 ft. 4 in. to 3 ft.; sometimes divided by a parting into two seams,	0	2	5
Strata, from 4 fms. to 7 fms.,	6	0	0
Splint Coal; extensively worked; varies in thickness from 8 ft. to 5 ft. 3 in.,	0	4	3
Strata, from an inch to 3 fms.,	1	3	0
Virgin, Wee, or Sourmilk Coal; varies in thickness from 1 ft. 6 in. to 2 ft. 8 in.; worked chiefly in the northern part of the basin; sometimes coalesces with the Splint coal so as to form with it a seam 7 ft. in thickness,	0	2	3
Strata, from 9 fms. to 14 fms.,	12	0	0
Airdrie Blackband Ironstone; varies from 1 ft. or so to 1 ft. 6 in.; worked chiefly in northern part of basin,	0	1	4
Strata, from 12 fms. to 21 fms.,	16	0	0
Newarthill and Cleland Roughband (Ironstone); a local seam; from 2 in. to 8 in.,	0	0	6
Strata, from 9 in. to 2 fms.,	1	3	0
Virtuewell Coal; varies from 2 ft. to 2 ft. 6 in. [the same coal as the Benhar and Johnstone seam of "North-central Basin," and Diamond seam of "Falkirk and Slamannan Basin"]; worked pretty generally in the shallower parts of the basin,	0	2	4
Strata, from 3½ fms. to 5 fms.,	4	3	0
Bellside Ironstone; varies from 5 in. to 9 in.; a local seam, worked only at Greenhill and Bellside, east of Newarthill and Cleland,	0	0	8
Strata, from 11 fms. to 13 fms.,	12	0	0
Kiltongue Musselband Ironstone and Oil Shale; worked chiefly in the Airdrie district; varies from 1 ft. 4 in. to 1 ft. 8 in.,	0	1	3
Strata, from 4 fms. to 7 fms.,	5	3	0

	Fms.	Ft.	In.

Kiltongue Coal ; worked chiefly in Airdrie and Coatbridge district; varies in thickness from 2 ft. 6 in. to 6 ft.; occasionally splits up into two or more seams with thin partings between them; same seam as Castlehill 1st seam (Carluke, Sheet 23); [at Calderbank a blackband ironstone, 9 ins., with associated "gas" and "free" coal (known as "Calderbraes" and "Kenuelburn" ironstone), occupies the position of the Kiltongue coal], . . .   **0   3   6**
    Strata, from 4½ fms. to 7 fms., ...   **5   3   0**

Upper Drumgray ; same seam as "Furnace coal" of Shotts, "Coxroad coal" of Slamannan, &c., and "Castlehill 2d seam" (Sheet 23); very little worked; varies from 1 ft. or less to 2 ft. 6 in., ...   **0   2   0**
    Strata, from 4 fms. to 10 fms., ...   **6   3   0**

Lower Drumgray ; same seam as "Smithy coal" of Shotts, "Low Coxroad or Balmoral Coal" of Slamannan, &c., and "Castlehill 3d seam" (Sheet 23); sparingly worked in north and north-east portions of the basin ; varies from 2 ft. to 2 ft. 8. in.,   **0   2   3**
    Strata, from 35 fms. to 45 fms., containing several thin seams of coal, none of workable thickness, which are the representatives of the seams worked at Shotts and Fauldhouse,   **40   0   0**

Upper Slaty Ironstone, of Stepends and Loadmanford; same as "Bowhousebog" seam (Sheet 23); varies from 0 to 3 ft. 6 in.; a very irregular seam, but, say **0   1   2**
    Strata, from 16 fms. to 17 fms., ...   **16   3   0**

Lower Slaty Ironstone ; worked along the eastern margin of the basin, at Goodockhill near Salsburgh ; a very irregular seam, sometimes replaced by a thin coal; varies in thickness from 0 to 8 feet, thinning and thickening out often very rapidly in one pit-working,—say, ...   **0   1   10**

64. The Clyde basin is intersected by numerous faults (see par. 89), many of which coincide approximately with the strike of the strata, and thus have the effect of repeating the outcrops, as it were, again and again. A glance at the Map will show the same seams cropping out successively as the beds are traversed by the strike-faults. Thus the coals which crop at Tollcross are thrown down to the north by a great east and west dislocation, and they again rise to the surface north of Shettleston. The same phenomena are seen to still better advantage in the Coatbridge and Airdrie districts, the crops being repeated there at least five times by step faults. The basin is bounded to the north by a great fault, which has cut off the extension of the coal-bearing strata in that direction ; while a similar large fault brings down the Coal-measures against the igneous rocks of the Cathkin Hills. Intrusive sheets and dykes of igneous rock occur now and again, especially in the north and north-east parts of the basin. Where these rocks appear at the surface they are indicated by the dark crimson-lake colour, but in many cases the intrusive rocks do not show at the surface, and their existence is only known from their having been passed through in pits and borings. As a rule, the coals that occur in the vicinity of intrusive sheets have been rendered useless, overlying seams having usually suffered more than those which lie beneath the igneous masses. The vertical dykes have as a rule affected the coal-seams only to a trifling extent. Now and again what are called "wants" occur in the coals. These indicate, in some places, old water channels which existed at the time the coal was being accumulated ; in other places they point to the action of running water, which washed away the coal soon after it had been formed. The "wants" are usually composed of sandstone, clay, or shale. "Sand and clay dykes," again, are deep channels or ravines and gullies which have been excavated down through the strata from the surface, by the action of streams and rivers, at a comparatively recent

date, and which have subsequently been filled up with sand, clay, and other detritus (see par. 97).

2. The North-Central Basin.

65. This basin includes the coal-fields of the moory tracts to the north of Airdrie, and which we shall here call the coal-fields of Arden and Binniehill; of Shotts and Bowhousebog; of Benhar and Fauldhouse; and of Torbanehill and Armadale.

The Arden and Binniehill district forms the northern portion of this wide basin, and includes its deepest part, consequently there are some coals met with there which do not occur, as far as known, in any other sections of the basin. The following table gives the succession and average thicknesses of the strata and various seams :—

Section of Arden and Binniehill Mineral Field.

	Fms.	Ft.	In.
Strata, ...	16	0	0
Ell Coal, occurs only at Whiterig, near Arden, .	0	3	6
Strata, ...	20	0	0
Pyotshaw and Main Coal, only at Whiterig, . . .	0	9	0
Strata, ...	8	0	0
Humph Coal, 1 ft. 8 in. to 2 ft. 4 in.; occurs only at Whiterig and Arden,	0	2	0
Strata, ...	5	0	0
Splint Coal, at Whiterig, Arden, and Darngavel, 3 ft. 6 in. to 4 ft., ...	0	3	9
Strata, ...	1	0	0
Sourmilk Coal, at Whiterig, . . .	0	1	6
Strata, ...	8	0	0
Musselband Coal, at Whiterig, ...	0	3	3
Strata, ...	4	0	0
Blackband Ironstone, confined to western part of the field, .	0	1	0
Strata, ...	15	0	0
Virtuewell or Johnstone Coal, widely worked, . .	0	2	6
Strata, ...	7	0	0
Ladygrange Coal, worked in central and eastern parts of the field,	0	2	0
Strata, ...	8	0	0
Musselband Shale and Ironstone, worked chiefly in western part of field, ...	0	1	2
Strata, ...	7	0	0
Kiltongue Coal, sparingly worked both in west and east, sometimes split up into two seams, ...	0	2	0
Strata, ...	7	0	0
Upper Drumgray Coal, worked chiefly in central part of the field, where it is known as the "Splint coal,"	0	2	0
Strata, ...	7	0	0
Lower Drumgray, met with in west part of field, thin, . .	0	1	8
Strata, uncertain thickness—say	40	0	0
Slaty Ironstone (? Lower), only got at Staylee Glen, . . .	0	1(?)	0

66. The Coal-measures in the Shotts, Bowhousebog, Benhar, and Fauldhouse district are distinguished by the greater development of the coalseams lying between the Virtuewell Coal and the Slaty Ironstone, several seams in this portion being worked, which either do not appear or are too thin to pay the cost of working in the northern districts of the "central basin." The following tables show the general section, the thicknesses given being averages :—

Section of the Shotts and Bowhousebog Mineral Field.

	Fms.	Ft.	In.
Benhar or Virtuewell Coal,	0	3	6
Strata,	7	0	0
Ladygrange Coal,	0	1	6
Strata,	11	0	0
Kiltongue Musselband,		...	
Strata,	7	0	0
Kiltongue Coal, represented by a few inches only,	0	0	4
Strata,	13	0	0
Shotts Furnace or Ball Coal (Upper Drumgray),	0	2	6
Strata,	6	3	0
Shotts Low Coal,	0	2	0
Strata,	7	0	0
Shotts Smithy Coal (Little or Lower Drumgray),	0	1	8
Strata,	6	0	0
Shotts Gas Coal,	0	3	0
Strata,	8	0	0
Clefted Coal or Blackhall Parrot,	0	3	0
Strata,	24	0	0
Liquo Coal,	0	1	7
Strata, variable thickness,	16	0	0
Bowhousebog Coal,	0	5	0
Strata, variable thickness,	2	3	0
Bowhousebog or Upper Slaty Ironstone,	0	1	0
Strata, variable thickness,	10	0	0
Lower or Crofthead Slaty Ironstone, position of.			

Section of Benhar and Fauldhouse Mineral Field.

	Fms.	Ft.	In.
Benhar or Virtuewell Coal,	0	4	0
Strata,	9	0	0
Ladygrange Coal,	0	1	0
Strata,	12	0	0
Kiltongue Musselband,	0	0	6
Strata,	7	0	0
Kiltongue Coal,	0	0	4
Strata,	15	0	0
Ball Coal (Shotts Furnace or Upper Drumgray Coal),	0	2	3
Strata,	7	0	0
Shotts Low Coal,	0	1	8
Strata,	6	0	0
Shotts Smithy Coal,	0	1	8
Strata,	5	0	0
Shotts Gas Coal,	0	2	6
Strata,	15	0	0
Mill Coal or Crofthead 4 ft. Coal,	0	3	0
Strata,	8	0	0
Coal (Coalinshields Seam),	0	2	4
Strata,	5	0	0
Coal (Armadale Main Seam),	0	2	0
Strata,	10	3	0
Coal (Coalinburn Seam),	0	1	10
Strata,	12	0	0
Slaty Ironstone (Lower or Crofthead and Goodockhill Seam),	0	0	10

67. The mineral seams worked in the Torbanehill and Armadale district, which lies immediately west of Bathgate, belong to the lower section of the Coal-measures, the highest coal met with being the Rough Parrot, which is the same seam as the Shotts Gas Coal. The strata immediately underlying the Coalinburn coal appear to be very variable. It is notice-

able that this is generally the case with those parts of the Carboniferous formation that contain seams of cannel coal and blackband ironstone. They thicken and thin out rapidly, and the associated seams of coal and ironstone are apt in the same way to change suddenly. The thicknesses given in the subjoined table are, as before, averages :—

Section of Torbanehill and Armadale Mineral Field.

	Fms.	Ft.	In.
Upper Cannel or Rough Parrot (Shotts Gas coal), . . .	0	2	6
Strata (a black shale in this series has been partially worked for gas and oil), ...	17	0	0
Mill Coal, ...	0	2	8
Strata, ...	8	0	0
Ball Coal or Coalinshields Coal and Ironstone. (The ironstone rests upon the coal, and varies from an inch up to 6 or 7 ft.; sometimes it is altogether wanting, ...	0	2	8
Strata, ...	4	8	0
Main Coal, ...	0	3	0
Strata, ...	10	0	0
Coalinburn Coal, ...	0	2	0
Strata, ...	0	4	0
Boghead or Torbanehill Parrot Coal, ...	0	0	8
Strata, ...	0	2	6
Blackband Ironstone, ...	0	0	8

68. The Map does not show so many faults in the North-central basin as are indicated within the area of the Clyde basin. But this is chiefly owing, no doubt, to the fact that much of the former basin has not yet been proved by pit-workings. In the districts which have been so proved faults occur in considerable numbers. The main faults run from west to east, and from north of west to south of east. North-east and south-west faults are of rare occurrence, and of inconsiderable importance. The strata are here and there cut by vertical dykes of basalt rock (see par. 85), while intrusive sheets of the same rock cover wide areas. Denudation has exposed large masses of these rocks, as in Torrance Hills, Cant Hills, Eastcraig Hills, &c., but large sheets lie buried at various depths, and have been passed through in trial borings. The coals, as already stated, are usually destroyed in the neighbourhood of these basalts; sometimes, however, where the influence of the molten rock has not been excessive, the coals are rendered somewhat anthracitic, and become useful for steam purposes. This is the case with the Splint or steam coal of Westfield, Meadowfield, &c. (Arden and Binniehill mineral field), and to some little extent with the Furnace coal of Shotts, where it adjoins the Cant Hills.

3. Grangemouth, Carron, Falkirk, and Slamannan Coal-Fields.

69. In spite of the strip of Millstone Grit which cuts across the Coalmeasures north of Falkirk and Camelon, the portion lying to the north of this interruption presents a section so nearly the same as that on the south side, that all the fields in this portion of the district may be conveniently taken together as one area, comprising all the Coal-measures from the north edge of the sheet south to the basalt dyke which bounds the Slamannan coal-field. The relation of the coal-seams and other economic minerals to the each other in the northern part of the area is shown in the following generalised table.

Section of Falkirk Coal-Field.

	Fms.	Ft.	In.
Strata,	2	0	0
Ironstone 2 in., Parrot Coal 3 in., Blaes 3 in., Coal 1 ft. 2 in.,	0	1	10
Strata,	0	1	6
Four-Foot, Cockmalane, or Diamond Coal (Virtuewell Coal),	0	4	0
Strata,	3	0	0

Oil Shale, . . 2 0
Parrot Coal, . 0 2
Ironstone, . . 0 3
Blaes, . . 0 6
Coal, . . 0 2

	Fms.	Ft.	In.
(above Oil Shale group)	0	3	1
Strata,	5	0	0
Coal, .	0	1	4
Strata,	7	0	0

Miller or Carron Two-ft. Coal, { Shell bed, . . 1 4 ; Blaes and Ironstone, 1 0 ; Coal, . . . 1 6 }

	Fms.	Ft.	In.
Miller or Carron Two-ft. Coal,	0	3	10
Strata,	10	0	0
Craw Coal, with 6 inches parting,	0	3	6
Strata,	7	0	0
Shell or Musselband,	0	1	0
Strata,	2	0	0
Splint or Main Coal (Kiltougue Coal),	0	3	0
Strata with about 8 fathoms of sandstone,	2	0	0
Coxroad or Soft Coal,	0	2	6
Strata, . } (Drumgray Coals),	3	0	0
Low Coxroad or Balmoral Coals, }	0	2	0
Strata with 6½ fathoms sandstone,	15	0	0

Auchingane Coal (Shotts Parrot Coal) { Ironstone Clayband, 0 4 ; Blaes, 0 6 ; Ironstone B. band, 0 6 ; Parrot Coal, 0 8 ; Soft Coal, 1 2 }

	Fms.	Ft.	In.
Auchingane Coal (Shotts Parrot Coal)	0	3	2
Strata containing a sandstone of 4 fathoms,	9	0	0
Blaes with two ribs of Clayband ironstone,	0	4	6
Brighton Main Coal, with two ribs of stone,	0	5	0
Strata chiefly sandstone,	4	0	0
Glenfuir or Gutterhole Coal, with 6 inches stone,	0	3	6
Strata,	1	2	0
Coal, .	0	1	0
Strata chiefly sandstone,	4	0	0
Coal, .	0	1	0
Strata,	0	1	0
Ironstone B. band,	0	0	3
Blaes, .	0	2	0
Ironstone B. band,	0	0	4
Blaes, .	0	1	11
Ironstone C. band,	0	0	2
Blaes, .	0	0	2
C.B. Ironstone, .	0	0	6
Strata,	0	2	4
Bonnyhill Upper Stone (Clayband), .	0	0	4
Fireclay,	0	2	3
Bonnyhill Upper Stone Coal, .	0	1	0
Strata, including 3 fathoms sandstone, .	3	3	9
Bonnyhill Craw Coal,	0	1	0
Strata,	1	0	0
Ballstone (Clayband), .	0	0	6
Strata, including 2 fathoms sandstone,	3	1	0

Ironstone B. band, 1 9
Daugh, . 0 3 } Stalyband Ironstone, . 0 3 2
Ironstone B. band, 1 2

70. It may be remarked generally of the Coal-measures in this area that the sandstones have their greatest development among the lower members of the formation, whence we may infer that at the time of their deposit the conditions under which the Millstone Grit had been formed still continued. Together with the presence of thick sandstone, it is also observable that the coal-seams in this lower part of the series are variable, both as regards their thickness and horizontal extent. The Slaty-band ironstone also, so useful as a horizon for the base of the Coal-measures, is remarkably lenticular, being found very thick in small patches which thin out in all directions, and at times cease altogether, reappearing, however, at no great distance on the same horizon, and then repeating the same behaviour. It would appear as if the animals whose remains have been mainly instrumental in the precipitating of this ironstone lived in more or less disconnected pools on the surface of the sandbanks which now form the Millstone Grit.

71. The Slaty-band ironstone has been much sought after, especially on the western margin of the area. From its lenticular character, however, much loss and disappointment have been incurred. The search for it requires constant boring, and only when a thick patch is lighted on is a good return obtained for the heavy outlay. Overlying this ironstone occurs a zone of rocks a few fathoms thick, very variable in their nature, but often containing numerous coal-seams and thick bands of clay ironstone. These last have been extensively wrought, each ironstone taking its name from some peculiarity it exhibits, and giving a name to the nearest coal; as, for instance, the "ballstone" and "speckle ball," the former name referring to the nodular character of the ironstone, the latter to the spotted or speckled appearance of a fractured surface, owing to the occurrence of iron pyrites throughout the stone. The famous Boghead coal of Bathgate occurs in this horizon, but does not seem to extend into this district. All the coals beneath the Coxroad or Drumgray seams are variable, and of poor quality. The last-named seams are extensively mined, and much sought after, the upper one being a caking coal. The Splint or Kiltongue coal is also in much request, being well adapted for furnace purposes. It has a very characteristic shell band above it. The uppermost coal of the series here is the Diamond, Cockmalome, or Virtuewell coal, an excellent house coal, covering, however, but a small area, and now only worked at Blackbraes. The Carron Two-foot and Craw coals, together with the most of the other seams of the field, are worked by the Carron Company for their furnaces, for which purpose alone they appear fitted. The "Miller" or Carron Two-foot coal has an oil shale, and sometimes an ironstone along with it.

72. In the southern or Slamannan portion of the area the general succession of strata closely resembles that in the Falkirk field, as is evident from the subjoined table:—

Section of the Slamannan Coal-Field.

		Ft.	in.	Fms.	Ft.	In.
Strata,				19	0	0
Johnstone or Virtuewell Coal { Shale,		0	8			
Ironstone,		0	2	0	3	8
Coal,		2	10			
Strata,				7	0	0
Lady Grange Coal,				0	2	8
Strata,				2	0	0
Coal,				0	1	1
Strata,				15	0	0

		Fms.	Ft.	In.
Shale or Mussel Ironstone—Fire-clay and Coal,	.	0	1	9
Strata, ...		4	0	0
Shale band, ...	.	0	1	2
Strata, . . .		0	2	6
Splint Coal (Kiltongue Coal),	.	0	1	10
Strata, . . .		14	0	0
Coxroad Coal, . .		0	1	10
Strata, . .		5	0	0

	Ft.	In.			Fms.	Ft.	In.
Shale, . .	0	9½	Balmoral or Low	Drumgray			
B. Band Ironstone,	0	3	Coxroad Coal.	Coals,	0	4	1½
Clear Coal, .	2	6					
Poor B. Band,	0	7					
Strata, .			.	.	11	0	0

	Ft.	In.			Fms.	Ft.	In.
Ironstone, .	0	1	Auchingane Coal, .	.	0	1	3½
Coal, .	1	2½					
Strata, .					3	0	0
Coal, .					0	0	8
Strata, .					15	0	0
Coal, .					0	0	7
Strata,					5	0	0
Coal, .					0	0	4
Strata, .					3	0	0
Coalblind, .					0	1	1
Strata,					8	0	0

73. In the southern area the position of the slaty band ironstone has not been reached. There appears, indeed, to underlie the whole field a great platform of intrusive basalt-rock, which is seen to emerge from the position of the Coxroad coal into that series of hills which forms the eastern edge of the Slamannan coal-field, dividing it from those of Bathgate and Shotts. This sheet seems not to keep one definite horizon; for where it appears again in the neighbourhood of Salsburgh and Shotts, it overlies the position of the Coxroad coals. It exerts a considerable influence on the coals in the Slamannan district, the Coxroad coal being in places, especially in the eastern part of the field, either rendered useless or having its caking quality impaired. The splint coal at Drumclair is converted into a hard steam coal resembling anthracite. Towards Lodge, on the western boundary of the field, the intrusive sheet of basalt shows indications that it lies on a lower horizon than on the east. The Virtuewell, or, as it is here locally termed, the "Johnstone Coal," though in this area a coarse splinty coal, has often a bed of oil shale and a black-band ironstone in connection with it, which cause it to be extensively mined. In the Slamannan coal-field a "want" occurs in the Splint coal seam. A blank space in that bed has been traced for about two miles in the workings. It runs approximately east and west with a somewhat bent course. The breadth of the actual blank space is not easily known, for mining operations are put a stop to as soon as the coal thins out so as no longer to be worked to profit. The explanation of this structure appears to be that during the formation of the material which went to make the coal, a water-course traversed the area in the direction of the want, and removed the decaying vegetable matter so as to expose the bed of clay on which it rested before the change of conditions took place, which brought in the sediment now forming the roof of the coal. The beds which elsewhere form the roof and pavement of the coal come together where the coal has disappeared.

74. This extensive mineral field is much broken by faults, and traversed by large basalt dykes which run approximately east and west. A peculiar feature of the great fault which cuts the coal-field south of Slamannan, is

that it now holds a basalt dyke between its walls. The dislocation may be inferred to be older than the great basalt sheet which underlies the field, seeing that the mass of igneous rock stops abruptly and does not occur again to the north of the line of fault. The basalt dyke in the Carron and Grangemouth fields is also accompanied by a displacement of the strata. In both cases the molten matter which formed the dykes probably rose along a reopened pre-existing fault.

75. The Coneypark and Banknock basin comprises a small area of Coal-measures, let down among the Carboniferous Limestone and Millstone Grit rocks by two nearly parallel faults, and measures between two and three square miles in extent. Though small in size it is rich in coal-seams. Owing to the effect of the boundary faults, beds much higher in the Coal-measures than any now existing north of the great Slamannan dyke have been thrown in and preserved in this little basin. These rocks may be identified with some of the higher seams in the main Lanarkshire coal-field. This is very interesting, as it shows the former extension of those beds, and of the Upper Red Sandstones, over districts from which they have been entirely removed by denudation.

Section of the Coneypark Coal-Field.

		Fms.	Ft.	In.
Upper or Red Coal-Measures. Red Sandstone,		6	0	0
Coal,		0	3	0
Strata,		23	0	0
Coneypark Thick Coal, { These beds are considered to be the same as the Pyotshaw and Main of Airdrie.		1	1	0
Fire-clay,		0	2	6
Coneypark Main Coal,		0	4	0
Strata,		7	3	0
Coal,		0	3	0
Strata,		5	0	0
Foul Coal,		0	4	6
Strata,		3	0	0
Coal,		0	3	6
Strata,		8	0	0
Coal,		0	1	6
Strata,		23	0	0
Coal Measures, Coal (Highest wrought in Banknock Old Coal-field)		0	1	6
Strata,		6	3	0
Five-Quarter Coal (Virtuewell or Cockmalane),		0	3	9
Strata,		14	0	0
Coal (Carron Two-foot Coal, "Miller" Coal of Falkirk, M'Neish of Clackmannan),		0	2	0
Strata,		5	0	0
Banknock Main Coal (Carron "Craw Coal"),		0	5	0
Strata,		12	0	0
Coal (Splint or Kiltongue Coal),		0	2	0
Strata,				
Drumgray Coal,				
Strata,				
Slaty Band Ironstone,				

76. Though this coal-field is now known to belong to the Coal-measures, yet, from its curious position among much older beds, and the difficulty of correlating its seams with those of the neighbourhood, it was once looked upon as an anomaly. Most of the seams have now been worked out, especially at the western end of the field, where they are most numerous, and the basin narrowest. When these mining operations took place the value of oil shale was not recognised; for a rich shale which accompanied

the Musselband coal was left untouched during the removal of the coal. Its value, however, is now fully appreciated, and the shale is being taken out also.

Igneous Rocks.

77. Igneous rocks are usually classed under two groups—one of which comprises those rocks which are of the same age as the strata with which they are interbedded ; while the other includes all those that are younger than the strata amongst which they have been intruded. Hence the former are termed *interbedded* or *contemporaneous*, and the latter *intrusive* or *subsequent*. Both groups are well represented in the present Map.

I. INTERBEDDED OR CONTEMPORANEOUS.

78. The rocks belonging to this group have already been described in connection with the Calciferous Sandstone (see pars. 18, 20, 22) and Carboniferous Limestone series (see par. 25-32). They are true volcanic rocks, having been ejected from volcanic orifices at the surface as masses of molten matter and showers of dust and stones, which subsequently became covered up by later deposits of aqueous origin. The volcanic rocks of the Campsie Hills, Kilsyth Hills, and Cathkin Hills have been shown to have been erupted during the time of the Calciferous Sandstone series. They are contemporaneous with similar rocks, comprising the great bank of volcanic origin which ranges westward to the Clyde at Dumbarton, and stretches through Ayrshire and Renfrewshire to the high grounds between the Rivers Avon and Irvine. Later in date come the igneous rocks of the Bathgate Hills. The lower and older portion of these may be assigned to higher parts of the Calciferous Sandstones, while the main mass continued to be erupted during the deposition of nearly the whole of the Carboniferous Limestone series. No higher interbedded igneous rocks occur in this region. Most of the intrusive masses, however, may be assigned to various dates long after the extinction of the Bathgate volcanoes.

II. INTRUSIVE OR SUBSEQUENT.

79. Though rocks of this series do not of themselves afford proof of their age, some indication of their date may now and then be obtained from the geology of the country surrounding them. In the present Map it is evident that many of them must be of later date than the Coal-measures ; and even those which traverse only the Carboniferous Limestone or Millstone Grit may nevertheless be of as recent date. A convenient classification ranges these rocks into two groups—1st, Those which occur as intrusive sheets or bosses ; and 2d, Those which traverse the other rocks as wall-like masses or dykes.

80. 1. *Intrusive Sheets.*—If we take a general view of the distribution of the intrusive sheets, we find them to belong to at least two platforms —(a) A series of sheets which have been injected among the lower portions of the Carboniferous Limestone series ; (b) A much more extensive and incursive set, ranging on different horizons from about the middle of the Millstone Grit upward into the heart of the Coal-measures. None of them have been noted here among the Upper Red Sandstone group which forms the highest member of the Carboniferous system.

81. The intrusive character of the basalt sheets is determined by the facts, that the same mass is found transgressively passing across different horizons of the strata between which it lies, and that the strata overlying these sheets may be observed to have been more or less strongly heated

and altered. These facts cannot indeed be always ascertained, for sections often fail at the very places where the evidence should occur; but they may be proved in so many instances, that there can be no doubt as to the necessity of classing the whole of these masses as intrusive. Petrographically, they may be described as varieties of basalt, passing into coarsely crystalline doleritic masses on the one hand, and on the other into dull, dirty green diabase. The sheets which in the Kilsyth and Denny district run through the lower portion of the Carboniferous Limestone series present considerable diversities of texture and composition even within comparatively short distances. While they consist normally of crystalline mixtures of triclinic felspar, augite, titaniferous iron or magnetite, and apatite, they now and then contain much orthoclase in well-developed Carlsbad twins, and also free quartz in minute blebs, evidently of original segregation, and not of secondary formation. Thus in some places, as in the Carron Water, the rock assumes a coarsely crystalline texture, and, from the pink tint of the felspar, resembles some of the so-called "syenites." A sample of this rock from Carron Water shows, under the microscope, a thoroughly crystalline texture, and consists of much kaolinized and ferruginized felspar, chiefly orthoclase, in Carlsbad twins; much titaniferous iron and apatite, with a little augite and quartz; the felspar is crowded with apatite prisms; the quartz contains vapour cavities and microlites; many of the crystals of titaniferous iron enclose granules of pyrites. To this rock the name of quartziferous diabase would be most appropriate. When we reflect that these large intrusive sheets have replaced large masses of stratified rock, much of which, no doubt, was actually melted up in their mass, we should be prepared for considerable local differences in the composition of such sheets. In particular, it may be surmised that the small blebs of quartz so frequent in some parts of the rock have been derived from arenaceous strata involved in the molten lava as it rose upwards.

82. The amount of alteration effected by these sheets, though sometimes considerable, seldom extends many yards from their edges. It varies both in kind and in degree, according to the character of the material on which the heated mass of the igneous rock has acted. Especially great has been the havoc produced among the coal-seams. Many of these have been entirely consumed, and their position is now occupied by igneous rock. Often the coals near a basalt are converted into a soft sooty substance, or a kind of coke; at other times, however, where the heat derived from the old molten rock has not been in excess, the coals have only been to a certain extent de-bituminised and converted into a kind of anthracite. In such cases the alteration has been due to the presence of a thick mass of igneous rock, generally underlying and separated from the coal by a considerable thickness of strata,—as much as 15 fathoms in some places. In close contact with a coal the basalt-rocks almost invariably assume a dirty grey or yellow colour, and become soft and clay-like in texture. At their junction with shales and sandstones some change in colour also takes place, but it is usually not so marked. The contiguous shales and sandstones themselves are often highly baked, the shales being porcellanised, and the sandstones cracked and hardened.

83. (a) The intrusive sheets in the Carboniferous Limestone series run as a ragged belt from near Kirkintilloch to beyond Stirling. They consist of various basalt and diabase rocks, which weather spheroidally on exposure. Their truly intrusive nature is made remarkably clear on the present Map. Reference has already been made (par. 43) to the intrusive mass which alters the Hurlet Limestone in the Carron Water, above Denny, where the limestone

'was said to overlie the basalt, and yet within a few yards to be replaced or cut out by it. Proceeding northward before we reach the Bannock Burn (Sheet 39), the Hurlet Limestone is seen to emerge from beneath the basalt, being much altered in connection with it, while from the Bannock Burn to Causewayhead, north of Stirling, a considerable thickness of sandstones and shales intervenes between the two rocks. Again the disruptive character of that great sheet of basalt on which the village of Kilsyth stands is equally evident. As in the case of the Denny sheet, it does not remain on one horizon of the sedimentary rocks into which it has thrust itself. Towards its eastern extension it lies about 70 or 80 fathoms below the Index Limestone, while at Croy it overlies it. At Kilsyth and Queenzie Burn, about 2 miles to the west, the limestone is found just on the top of the basalt; while at the latter place, where there is an exposure of the junction of the two rocks in the burn, the limestone is found to be much altered. In the Croy district, the sheet of basalt, which on each side lies between sedimentary strata, suddenly leaves one horizon, passes up vertically between the broken edges of the beds, and re-enters a higher one. There is no trace of a fault at this place; on the contrary, the strata lie quite undisturbed, as has been proved by the mining operations which have been carried on beneath. These sheets of basalt, together with some others in the same district, seem to have been intruded among the Carboniferous rocks before these were much disturbed, as they are folded and faulted in the same manner as the sedimentary strata among which they occur.

84. (*b*) The intrusive basalt sheets in the Millstone Grit and Coal-measures form another broken band across the centre of this Map. Some of considerable size occur immediately to the east of Glasgow, at Gartcraig, Cardowan, &c. Numerous smaller patches also appear scattered along the boundary of the Clyde basin and the North-central basin at New Monkland, Rawyards, Moffat, &c. Some of the largest sheets, however, are met with in the North-central basin, near Hillend Reservoir, Torrance, Kirk of Shotts, Blairmuckhill, Eastcraighill, &c. Another large sheet, intruded among strata belonging to both the Millstone Grit and Limestone series, extends from Torphichen northwards for two miles.

85. 2. *Dykes.*—One of the most conspicuous features on the Map is the series of long east and west lines of crimson, which are there made to traverse indifferently all the geological formations. These are dykes of basalt, varying in thickness from a few feet up to 50 yards or more. They cut across all the rocks up to the drift series, and are later than any known fault or dislocation, since they traverse faults equally with the strata that are faulted. They have thus been inferred to belong to the Miocene period. (Explanation to Sheet 14, par. 63). They consist of a dark blue, greenish, or black crystalline basalt, more or less homogeneous in character. Now and again they are sparingly amygdaloidal in the centre. At their junction with the rocks they traverse there is seldom much disturbance or alteration—the amount of either apparently bearing some relation to the breadth or thickness of the dyke. Thus, small dykes seem to affect the strata to a less extent than large ones. Their general trend in the present area is east and west. As a rule, their course is approximately straight, and this is particularly the case when they traverse the more yielding strata of sandstone, shale, &c. When they traverse harder rocks, however, their course is not infrequently rapidly undulating. This appearance is much better shown in other districts which have been examined by the Geological Survey; but an illustration is afforded on the present Map by the great dyke that traverses the Campsie Hills and Kilsyth Hills eastward to the Carron coal-field. Five main dykes are shown upon the Map. One of these, which cuts across

the North-central basin, is interrupted at Chryston, but reappears a little to the north of its former position. No trace of it appears at the surface between Chryston and Knockmilly, but it is probably continuous below ground. It is not uncommon indeed to meet with dykes which terminate upwards. In some coal-pits such dykes are found to intersect the lower seams, while the upper seams are continuous, and show no trace of the dyke that occurs below.

86. Near Black Braes, south-east from Falkirk, two of the large dykes overlap each other and end off in sharp points. There is every reason to believe, however, that these two are in reality one dyke with an underground connection between them. Mining operations seem to corroborate this supposition. Many small dykes occur in the area of the Coal-measures, as at Shettleston, Swinton, Bredisholme, Bonnybridge, &c.; similar short dykes have been traced in the limestone areas, as seen at Kilsyth and in the Bathgate Hills. Some of these dykes may extend for much greater distances than are shown upon the Map, as our knowledge of them is only derived, in many cases, from pit-workings—the dykes not appearing at the surface of the ground.

87. Dykes may or may not coincide with faults. Sometimes they run for many miles along a line of dislocation, as in the case of the great dyke that stretches from Cadder to Torphichen. In most instances, however, the strata on the one side of a dyke correspond precisely with those on the other, showing that the dykes are not necessarily connected with those movements of the earth's crust that gave rise to the dislocation of the strata. (See par. 74).

Faults.

88. The faults which are shown upon this Map may be roughly classed under two divisions—1st, Faults that strike approximately west and east; and 2d, Faults that trend from north-west to south-east. Frequently, however, a fault may belong to both divisions—running for some distance in one direction and then turning off at an angle towards some other point in the horizon. Now and again, also, dislocations are found to strike at right angles or nearly so to both classes of faults just referred to. Such north and south and north-east and south-west faults, however, are as a rule of very minor importance—the most considerable example being that which separates the limestone series from the trappean masses of the Kilsyth Hills. This fault may indeed be looked upon as belonging to the east and west group, and the same may be said of the two large faults that form the boundaries of the small Banknock or Dennyloanhead coal-field. Faults appear to be most numerous in the coal-bearing districts, for the well-known reason that the strata in those districts have been most thoroughly explored by mining operations. By far the larger proportion of the dislocations represented upon the Map as occurring within these areas are not really visible at the surface, which is often densely obscured by drift deposits. It is highly probable that were the districts unproductive of useful minerals to become as well known as the present coal-fields, faults would prove to be no less numerous there. At present the only fractures to be detected in such districts are those exposed in natural or artificial cuttings, or whose presence may be inferred from other evidence at the surface.

89. In the Clyde basin all the more considerable faults, and the majority of the minor ones, whether east and west, or north-west and south-east dislocations, correspond in a rough way with the strike of the strata, although numerous small slips cut across the beds at all angles. One result of this is to repeat the crops of the strata again and again, and

thus to bring the same coals up to the surface several times. Faults of this kind are called step-faults. The Map shows the upper coal-seams cropping out from below the Red Sandstone group near Tollcross and Fullarton. From the general southerly dip the lower coals might have been expected to crop out towards the north, and by-and-by the Millstone Grit to appear, followed by the Limestone series. But owing to the large east and west fault near Shettleston, the red rocks and underlying coal-strata have been brought down, and the coals accordingly crop out again further to the north. This process is repeated at least six times, as the strata are followed towards the north-east, by which means the coals appear to be spread over a wider area than they would have occupied had no disloca-tions taken place. But if we cross the coal-basin in the opposite direc-tion, that is to say from its outskirts towards its central and deeper por-tions, then the step-faults will appear to us to have *brought up* instead of *having thrown down* the crops, and thus to have lessened rather than increased the area of coal-bearing strata. The faults of the Clyde basin vary in amount from mere shifts of a few feet up to vertical displace-ments of more than 300 fathoms. The dislocation that brings the coal strata down against the volcanic rocks of the Cathkin Hills can hardly be less than 400 fathoms in some places. The east and west throw, that runs east from Glasgow to Baillieston and Old Monkland, ranges from 100 fathoms to 145 fathoms, the shift being down to the north; and there are others not much inferior to this in extent. Faults of 20 fathoms to 40 fathoms are common; and smaller dislocations are still more numerous. Many of the minor faults indeed could not be shown upon the Map. Frequently faults split up or divide into a number of smaller dislocations; while in not a few cases one fault cuts off and sometimes intersects and displaces another. None of them ever gives rise to inequalities at the surface, save when it has been the means of bringing hard rocks into juxta-position with softer and more easily worked strata. In cases of this kind the hard rocks generally project above the general level of the ground; but the high ground is as often on the *low* side as on the *high* side of a fault. It will be seen that the faults intersect the Clyde and other water-courses at all angles, and have no immediate connection what-ever with the present configuration of the ground. These remarks apply generally also to the faults shown in the North-central basin. None of these exceeds 40 fathoms or 50 fathoms in amount. A large part of this basin, however, owing to the presence of massive sheets of igneous rock, has deterred mining operations, and consequently our knowledge of it is not so detailed as is the case with the Clyde basin.

90. In the northern half of the Map, including the Slamannan, Fal-kirk, and Grangemouth mineral fields, as well as the limestone districts of Lennoxtown, Kilsyth, and Denny, similar observations may be made regarding the twofold direction of the dislocations, though numerous examples occur not properly admissible either into the E. and W. or the S.E. and N.W. group. Those which run in the latter direction are pro-bably the older set. No very decided evidence on this point indeed can be gleaned from the country embraced within the present Sheet; but on the other side of the Forth, in the Clackmannan coal-field (Sheet 39), where the same system of fault is found, the east and west ones displace the others. The great east and west faults, with a downthrow to the north, have been adduced as evidence that the valley of the Forth has been pro-duced by the letting down of the strata by a series of step-faults, the dislocations in this area being looked on as those which produced the south side of the valley. A mere glance at the Map, however, will show that the greater number, as well as the more powerful of these faults, have their downthrow to the south, a fact which has been entirely ignored.

The truth is these faults, as has been above remarked, produce no features on the surface except where softer and harder beds are brought against each other by them, the latter, from their greater power of resisting the agents of waste, usually standing above the former. As in the Clyde valley, so in the area round Denny and Kilsyth, the water-courses run across these faults at almost right angles, while further to the east the trend of the streams, as well as the whole features of the ground, run obliquely to their direction and entirely independently of them.

Ice-worn Rocks and Drift.

91. *Ice-worn Surface of the Country.*—The greater proportion of the area represented on this Map is more or less covered with superficial deposits of clay, gravel, sand, &c. These accumulations lie thickest and form the most continuous sheets in the valleys and low grounds. Over the higher grounds they are not only thinner but much less continuous, appearing often in mere isolated patches. We may conceive of them as forming a ragged mantle that obscures the solid rocks at low levels, but allows the more prominent ridges and hills to protrude. The hilly tracts often exhibit the appearance of having been smoothed off in some determinate direction, presenting to the eye that flowing outline which is so characteristic of ground over which glacier-ice has passed. But distinctly-marked glacial striæ are not often visible on exposed and weathered rock surfaces. Where the turf or superficial deposits, however, have been recently removed, such ice-markings are as a rule conspicuous. The general trend of the striæ and groovings shows that the ice which covered the country has flowed on the whole in an easterly direction.

92. As might be expected, the most numerous instances of *roches moutonnées* occur in the more hilly districts, where the rock either protrudes naturally above the superficial accumulations, or where it has been laid bare by man. Excellent examples of this phenomenon occur on a ridge of bare Millstone Grit seen near Sauchierig, about four miles south-west from Falkirk. Numerous other instances of striation may be observed, especially in the neighbourhood of Denny, Kilsyth, and Slamannan. The direction of the striæ, as well as the "carry" of the debris, would tend to show that the ice entered the district from the north-west, and after crossing the high ground of the Campsie Fells, turned upon itself and flowed more or less east. Near Kilsyth the direction is E. 5° N.; about Falkirk E. 10°–15° N.; while near Slamannan the direction is E. 10°–15° S., as if there were a divergence in anticipation of the meeting with the Linlithgowshire Hills. The Cathkin Hills are likewise striated from W. by N. to E. by S. Near Kilsyth the great basalt sheet has been carved into a succession of parallel *roches moutonnées* in the direction of the ice-flow there. At a distance these have the characteristic smooth whale's-back contour, but on a nearer approach they are found to be strewn over with innumerable blocks of the same material as the rock beneath, evidently the result of weathering *in situ.* The blocks represent in fact the harder kernels from which successive decomposed shells of rock have exfoliated on exposure. The only part of the rock where striæ can at present be observed here is along the southern margin of the Townhead Reservoir.

93. The Drift Series of deposits consist of the following subdivisions:—

  a. Boulder-clay or Till.
  b. Sand and Gravel.
  c. Erratic Blocks.
  d. Terraces of erosion and deposit.

94. (a) *The Boulder Clay* varies a little in character throughout the area included in this Map, chiefly, however, in regard to colour. It is an unstratified amorphous accumulation of tough clay, through which are promiscuously scattered sub-angular, smoothed, and striated stones and boulders, in less or greater abundance. Its general colour in the Carboniferous tracts is dark dingy grey, blue, or almost black, but in the Red Sandstone area of the Clyde basin it assumes a reddish tinge; and the same is the case in the region of the Campsie and Kilsyth Hills. While the great proportion of the stones in the boulder clay are of local derivation, a small number may usually be counted bearing witness to a more distant transport. In the Campsie Hills, for instance, the reddish boulder clay is chiefly made up of the debris of the porphyrites comprising them, with an admixture of the Old Red Sandstone and Highland rocks which lie to the north-west of that range. Down on the Carboniferous plains, however, and especially in the neighbourhood of Falkirk and Slamannan, the boulder clay is evidently made up chiefly of abraded Carboniferous rocks, with comparatively few travelled stones, but enough to show that a portion of the materials has been brought from the north-west. The occurrence, therefore, of fragments of conglomerate, mica-schist, chlorite-slate, greywacke, gneiss, and other rocks in the boulder clay which are not found *in situ* within the area of this Map, but which have certainly been derived from the Old Red Sandstone and Highland tracts towards the north-west, taken along with the evidence of the striæ on the rocks below, demonstrates that the ice which glaciated those rocks and formed the boulder clay, flowed from the Highlands, crossing in its course the Hills of Menteith, the Bucklyvie Moors, and the Campsie Fells, and then spreading over the lower grounds in a general easterly direction. There is evidence, moreover, to show that in the valley of the Clyde the ice stream turned gradually away, first in a south-easterly, and afterwards in a south-westerly direction (see par. 93, Explanation to accompany Sheet 23). The boulder clay usually presents a softly undulating outline, and now and again the rounded banks which it forms are arranged more or less conspicuously in parallel lines. This is best seen in the district between Falkirk and Slamannan, and in the tract that stretches south from Kirkintilloch to the valley of the Clyde. The trend of these banks coincides in direction with that of the glaciation of the country—they run approximately west and east.

95. In the more hilly grounds, the boulder clay for the most part presents no trace of beds. On the plains, however, it often shows included strata. In the Forth Valley, especially near Grangemouth, several beds of sand and gravel are found intercalated between and alternating with boulder clay. The following sections will show this arrangement better than any description :—

No. 1. Section of Drift and Superficial Deposits at Town Croft, near Grangemouth.

		Fms.	Ft.	In.
	Surface soil,	0	4	0
Beds of 50 feet Beach,	Gravel,	0	0	9
	Blue mud and sand,	2	4	0
Glacial beds belonging to 100 feet Beach,	Gravel,	0	3	0
	Sand,	1	2	0
	Red clay and sand,	1	5	0
	Red clay (brick clay),	5	5	3
Boulder Clay,	Soft blue till,	6	2	0
	Sand,	0	1	0
	Hard blue till,	0	5	0
	Sand,	0	1	0
	Hard blue till,	5	1	0

D

No. 2. Section in Bore (No. 5), Town Croft, near Grangemouth.

		Fms.	Ft.	In.
	Surface soil,	1	0	0
50 feet Beach,	Blue mud,	0	3	0
	Shell bed,	0	1	0
	Gravel,	0	2	0
	Blue mud,	2	2	0
	Gravel,	0	3	0
100 feet Beach,	Blue mud and sand,	2	3	0
	Red clay and sand,	1	4	0
	Red clay,	8	1	0
Boulder Clay,	Blue till and stones,	3	2	0
	Sand,	3	2	0
	Hard blue till and stones,	4	0	0
	Sand,	0	2	0
	Hard blue till and stones,	6	4	0
	Sand,	1	1	0
	Hard blue till,	4	0	0

No. 3. Section at Langlee, near Carron Iron Works.

		Fms.	Ft.	In.
Carse Clays and alluvium,	Sand,	0	4	0
	Mud and sand,	3	0	0
100 feet Beach,	Red mud and yellow clay,	7	1	0
Boulder Clay,	Blue till and stones,	2	4	0
	Mud and quicksands,	12	1	0
	Blue till and stones,	0	3	0

96. In the central coal-field tracts also numerous sections of this kind have been met with, sometimes in natural and artificial cuttings at the surface, at other times in deeper mining operations. At Chapelhall, at a height of 526 feet above the sea, a bed of clay, intercalated between a lower and upper mass of boulder clay, has yielded arctic shells.[1] In the same neighbourhood, beds of fine gutta percha clay and sand, which have yielded layers of peat and terrestrial vegetable remains, have been found occupying a similar position;[2] and at Orbiston, there is a brick clay worked which also appears to belong to the "beds in the till." This brick clay contains hazel nuts.

97. Underneath the boulder clay, similar deposits of clay, sand, and gravel sometimes appear. Many of these deposits may occupy the sites of old lakes, while others certainly occur in what were once river beds and ravines. Several good examples have been discovered during the mining operations in the coal-fields. They are known to the miners as sand dykes and clay dykes, according to the nature of the material that fills them. The beds with vegetable remains at Chapelhall appear to occupy such an ancient water-course, the direction of which is indicated upon the Map by a double line, as running from east to west. Other excellent instances are met with in the neighbourhood of Cleland and Newarthill. One of these is shown upon the Map as beginning at Cleland Townhead, and running south to the valley of the Calder Water, which it crosses. The other appears on the north side of the Calder Water, about a mile or so further to the east. Neither the one nor the other forms any feature at the surface. They are both, however, seen in section—one in Tillon Burn, and the other in the banks of the Calder, near Wishaw House (see Explanation, Sheet 23, par. 95). The troughs are filled with sand and fine gravel, buried below a thick mass of tumultuous boulder clay. They probably represent the courses of the Tillon Burn and the Calder

[1] J. Smith of Jordanhill, *Researches in Newer Pliocene Geology*, pp. 17, 141; *Quart. Jour. Geol. Soc.* vol. xxi. p. 219; "Monograph of Post-Tertiary Entomostraca," *Palæontological Society*, vol. xxviii. p. 6.

[2] "On the phenomena of the Glacial Drift of Scotland," *Trans. Geol. Soc. Glasg.* vol. i. p. 61.

Water during pre-glacial and inter-glacial times.[1] Another sand dyke is shown upon the map as occurring at Midhill and Parkhead, one mile or so to the east of Newarthill. This is probably a continuation of one of the old troughs just referred to. It is impossible to tell, however, whether it is part of the old course of the Tillon Burn or the Calder Water. It is nowhere exposed at the surface.

98. Further examples of these buried river channels occur in the coal-fields further north. One of much interest has been traced from Grange-mouth westwards to Larbert Junction, and thence to Carmuirs and Bonnybridge. Its further course in that direction is not known, though it probably follows nearly the direction of the Bonny Water and the Forth and Clyde Canal.[2] Another buried rock trench, found beneath the allu-vium of the present Kelvin River, corresponds roughly with the present course of this stream from one mile south of Kilsyth to about Nether-wood, a distance of four miles in an E.N.E. direction. The trench here cuts obliquely across the anticline known as the " Riggin," with the axis of which it coincides for about one mile of its course. These ancient water-courses, especially that at Grangemouth, which is a long way below the present sea-level, would tend to show that the land stood higher in pre-glacial times than now.

99. (b) *Sand and Gravel, &c.*—These deposits occur here and there, and rest either upon the boulder clay or on solid rock. They consist, for the most part, of well water-worn materials, arranged more or less distinctly by water action. They all belong to a more recent date than the boulder clay. They are usually termed "kames," and commonly assume the form of knolls, hummocks, banks, ridges, cones, and mounds, and they occur at many different levels. Not unfrequently their distribution bears some relation to the configuration of the ground. Thus one set of gravel and sand mounds begins at Stane, about 750 feet above the sea, and continues down the valley of the South Calder Water as far as Allanton, where the knolls abruptly terminate at a height of 500 feet above the sea. A similar connection between the distribution of the kames and the form of the ground may be noted in the valley of the Couston Burn, near Bathgate.

100. The most important area of sandy drift within the area of the Map is that which extends, with a breadth of about 3 miles, westwards from Lithgow Bridge to Polmont Mill. It narrows to a point at Falkirk, where it is covered and obliterated by the 100 foot beach to be afterwards noticed. Emerging from this interruption, it passes up to Denny, and then swings round to follow the direction of the Bonny Water to Kilsyth. It is everywhere ridged into the characteristic kames and mounds. One ridge deserves special mention, from the fact that it runs as a conspicuous feature parallel with the Edinburgh and Glasgow Railway from Redding to the borders of Linlithgowshire, a distance of 3 to 4 miles. This is not its whole length, however, for it passes westward from Redding by Cal-lendar Park, where it is breached, to the town of Falkirk, which is built on it, and it runs eastward across the valley of the Avon, which has cut across it. Its entire length cannot be less than 8 miles. Near Slaman-nan a few kames are seen to protrude through the alluvium of the Avon. Another group occurs at a higher level near Denny.

101. Kames often lie on water partings, and other places far removed from present stream courses. In such positions they are composed some-times of very coarse materials—a mixture of sand and angular debris, which shows little or no trace of bedding. A good example of this kind occurs at the Fauldhouse Hills. Lines of kames likewise cross the water-sheds between the Buckie Burn, a tributary of the Carron, and the Ban-

---

[1] See *Trans. Edin. Geol. Soc.* vol. i. p. 345; *Great Ice Age*, p. 189.
[2] See paper by J. Croll, *Trans. Geol. Soc. Edin.* vol. i. p. 330.

nock Burn (Sheet 39). The upper limit of these seems to be about 1000 feet above the sea. Near the head of the Birken Burn, just below where it emerges from the reservoir to the north of Kilsyth, a platform of coarse gravel is found on the watershed, at an elevation of about 1500 feet.

102. (c) *Erratic blocks.*—Boulders which do not belong to the districts embraced in this Map are met with now and again at the surface. They may once have been more plentiful than they now are, but as most of the country has been for a long time under cultivation, few have been preserved. They consist in every instance of rocks which belong to the west and north-west of the region in which they occur, and fragments of the same rocks occur commonly enough in the boulder clay. Indeed, many of the erratics lying loose at the surface may have come out of that accumulation.

103. It is observable that large boulders of Highland rocks do not appear south of the Campsie Fells in such numbers as might have been expected from the many conspicuous blocks seen in the neighbourhood of Stirling (Sheet 39). Possibly the Campsie Hills may have intercepted them. Blocks of porphyrites from those hills are pretty well distributed to the south and east of that ground. Some of them attain a great size, one weighing over 80 tons. The most conspicuous erratic blocks are to be seen along the valley of the Kelvin and Bonny Water, where boulders of the Campsie volcanic rocks, and especially of the Kilsyth basalt, are distributed over the surface of the ground, and even the gravel kames are in places so covered by them that it is often difficult at first sight to discriminate between the gravel ridges and the long bare *roches moutonnées* of basalt already referred to, as occurring near Kilsyth. None of the blocks are found lying on the strata which make up the 100 feet beach, though these beds, as will be immediately shown, were deposited while arctic conditions still existed in the district. That many are buried up by these latter deposits is more than probable, for to the east of Falkirk large boulders of basalt are strewn on the bluff formed by the denudation of these beds and the underlying sands, gravels, and boulder clay when the flat of the Carse was being levelled out of them by the Forth estuary.

104. (d) *Terraces of erosion and deposit belonging to the Glacial Period.*—In the valley of the Clyde the deposits which overlie the boulder clay sometimes assume the form of broad terraces composed partly of sand and gravel, and partly of silt and laminated clay. They differ from the kames, which are totally unfossiliferous, in having yielded at one place (Uddingston) marine shells of arctic species. Otherwise, the deposits of this terrace appear to be quite unfossiliferous, and it is probable that the shell-bed referred to may be of older date than the terrace, and of the same age as the shelly brick clays which occur underneath the upper boulder clay in the lower reaches of the Clyde. (See par. 107.) The terrace in which the shells in question occur may be traced from near Hamilton (Sheet 23), along the south side of the valley down to within a short distance of Cambuslang. Its boundary is very well marked out by the contour line of 200 feet. On the north side of the river it forms an equally well-marked platform or terrace, which may be followed at nearly the same height down as far as Viewpark. After this its bounding-line gradually falls to about the 100 feet contour-line. Its surface is sometimes very level, at other times gently undulating. At and above Uddingston it is largely made up of clay, silt, and sand, but further down the valley its materials become coarser, and its surface more irregular, so that it passes, as it were, into a series of banks, hummocks, and heaps of gravel and sand, as at Drumsargad Castle and Daldowie.

105. (1) 100 Feet Terrace.—In the neighbourhood of Falkirk, skirting the low plain known as the "Carse," from which it is always

separated by a steep bluff or cliff, lies a flat terrace which begins near Laurieston, widens out towards Falkirk, and passes up to about Bonnybridge. The Carron and Bonny Waters have cut on this level tract deep and wide channels, on the floors of which they have laid down their own alluvial haughs. North of these streams the terrace reappears as a broad platform, on which the villages of Stenhouse Muir aud Larbert stand, and the famous Falkirk Trysts are held. It may be described as forming in a sense all the ground between the Scottish Central Railway and the Carse. This terrace appears to have originally sloped gently from its inland margin towards the Forth. Even now, though much cut up by the water-courses which trench it, it still, when viewed in certain directions, retains much of its primitive character, for these inequalities are then lost sight of. Its upper limit near Falkirk is bounded by the 100 foot contour-line, but when traced upwards towards Bonnybridge, it rises to about 120 feet above the sea-level. If followed into Sheet 39 in the neighbourhood of Stirling, this peculiarity is still more striking.

106. The strata composing this terrace consist chiefly of tough, finely levigated and well laminated, plastic brick clays, which have the appearance of sheets of gutta percha piled on each other. These clays usually form the base of the series, while above them come alternations of fine sands and bands of more sandy clay than the bottom beds. Near the margin of the terrace, beds of fine gravel often form the highest beds. That those deposits were accumulated under glacial conditions of climate may be inferred from the fact that among the lower brick clays, where scarce a grain occurs to roughen the extremely fine silt, a striated stone may now and then be detected. These extraneous fragments are from six to eight inches across, and look as they had been drifted away and dropped in by floating ice. The clays, too, seem to be made up of the flour of rocks— a true ice-formed mud carried from inland glaciers by streams and deposited in the quiet waters of the Firth. They are singularly devoid of organic matter and organisms. Such fossils as have been met with are of an arctic type. Bones of a seal were got at Grangemouth in an extension of these beds under the Carse, which Professor Turner thinks to be those of *Pagomys fœtidus*.[1] Among the beds which overlie the brick clay, several of the clay seams are crumpled up in a wonderful manner, great sheets of them being rolled over and over, and involving the associated sands for considerable horizontal distances, as evidenced by the sections in the railway cuttings at Larbert. This would seem to point to the stranding of sheet pack ice on the sand and mud banks of that period. The clays and sands of this terrace lie indiscriminately upon the older formations. Near Polmont they are found reposing on an eroded platform of boulder clay. At Falkirk they lap round and obliterate the kames of the sand and gravel series. At Larbert they again rest on the boulder clay, while near Hamilton Farm, north of that place, they lie on the bare rock. At Grangemouth and under the Carse generally they have boulder clay beneath them. It would seem that these beds were laid down when the land stood 100 feet below its present level, and that while the sea was eating into the land along its margin deposition was going on further to seaward.

107. Similar phenomena may be observed in the valley of the Clyde, where a corresponding well-marked terrace has been cut into the boulder clay, and the deposits by which that clay is overlaid. This terrace consists of accumulations of clay, sand, and gravel, lying on an eroded platform of boulder clay. Its surface is generally very level, and it reaches 100 feet over the sea. Its boundaries are indicated upon the Map by the green lines in the vicinity of Shettleston, Cambuslang, &c. At and below

[1] See *Proceedings of the Royal Society of Edinburgh* for 1869–1870, pages 105–114.

the level of this terrace brick clays are extensively worked in the neighbourhood of Glasgow. These clays, however, belong to the older drift series,—their true position being *in* the boulder clay, as is shown by their being covered here and there by broad sheets of boulder clay. They occur at or near the surface on the 100 feet terrace, simply because the boulder clay that once covered them has been largely denuded.

108. (2) **Fifty Feet Terrace or Raised Beach.**—This terrace forms the platform on which the "Carse" of Falkirk lies. It is bounded on the landward side by the bluff above referred to as always fringing the 100 feet beach, and at the seaward side by the recent mud of the Forth. Its upper limit, like that of the 100 feet beach, rises in level the further inland it is traced. In the present district it nearly coincides with the fifty feet contour-line. This wide flat is in great measure a platform cut out of the older drift deposits; and in some places, indeed, projecting ridges of the underlying rock have been reached. Over this platform has been spread a thin coating of dark mud and sand with beds of recent shells. These deposits become thicker as they recede from the bluff or old shore line towards the water. Many of the clays or muds among them are quite fœtid from the quantity of organic matter they contain. Layers of peaty matter are not of infrequent occurrence. Bones and antlers of red deer have been found in them. Both the present terrace, therefore, and that at a level of 100 feet are partly terraces of denudation and partly of deposition. Properly speaking, they are only raised beaches along their upper margins; their lower sloping surfaces mark the infra-littoral areas of their time.

109. A line of interesting kitchen-middens runs along the bluff for half a mile or so on either side of where the River Avon enters the Carse. A section across a heap fifty yards long by twenty wide was exposed in a road cutting, and showed many successive layers of shells—principally oysters—to a depth of three feet without the bottom being visible. The remains of fire places were plentiful among the shells. Oysters seem to have been preferred by the makers of the midden, though they had also used the *Anomia*, the big "horse mussel" (*Modiola*), the common mussel (*Mitylus edulis*), the whelk (*Buccinum undatum*), periwinkle (*Littorina littorea*). Fragments of the large edible crab (*Cancer Pagurus*) were also present. All the valves of the oyster were separate except such as had been empty, and which still had barnacles or zoophytes in their interior. The mussel and other shells were found in separate nests, and not indiscriminately throughout the mound. Layers of sand were also found among the shells. All the middens observed occur on the bluff itself or just at its base, as if, when it was the limit of high water, the people who formed the middens, after searching the shores during low water, had retreated thither to enjoy their feast while the tide covered their hunting ground. The presence of the middens in this situation, taken in connection with the canoes and rude weapons found near the whale's skeleton in the Carse clays near Stirling, would tend to point to the upheaval of the Carse since the occupation of the country by man. Few or no oysters are now found in the Forth above Borrowstounness.

Alluvium—Peat.

110. *Alluvium.*—The low tracts bordering either side of the River Forth above Borrowstounness, are alternately covered and laid bare by the tide. At low water they show a great breadth of dark unctuous estuarine mud. By means of turf dykes and self-acting sluices a considerable portion of this ground has been reclaimed from the estuary into good arable land, and more work of the same kind might be done with advantage.

Considerable belts of alluvium fringe the larger streams which enter the area of the Map, and from the characteristic "haughs." In the case of the Clyde, the river winds through an alluvial plain of its own making, sometimes exceeding a mile in breadth. The Kelvin likewise has cut out a broad channel through the drift deposits, and laid down a wide but sinuous band of alluvium. This stream, from Castlecary to Kilsyth, appears to have at one time flowed through a chain of small lakes, and to have gradually silted them up. The River Avon, near Slamannan, seems to have had a similar history. Many of the streams show successive traces of alluvium at different heights, the uppermost being of course oldest. These older river plains commonly exist in very fragmentary forms, seeing that they are cut away during the gradual erosion of their valleys. Such fragments as could be expressed upon the scale of this Map will be found marked along the river margins. Near Bothwell, on the Clyde, for example, fragments of three successive terraces rise above the modern alluvium of the river. Perhaps the Carron, better than any other stream within the area of the Map, illustrates the erosive and reproductive action of a river. Together with its tributary the Bonny Water, it has excavated a deep trench, partly through solid rock, and partly, in its lower reaches, through the older marine terraces and the drifts. The curious mounds known as the "Hills of Dunipace" are monuments of this erosion, for they can be identified as portions of the 100 foot terrace left standing in midst of the valley which has been cut away around them. The Carron flowed originally on the top of this terrace. By degrees it has cut its way down to a depth of fully 80 feet below that former level. The Hills of Dunipace, no doubt, rose in one or more of the loops or "links" of the river, and keeping that position while the river curved all round and between them, they have succeeded in escaping destruction. Of its progress the river has left behind other memorials, in the form of successive terraces marking stages in the erosion of the valley and in the deposit of the alluvium. Four such river beds may be seen one above another near Dorrator. One of them may show the level at which the river ran during the formation of the fifty-foot beach. Since the elevation of the land the river has cut beneath the level of the surrounding Carse lands, and laid out still lower flats of alluvium down to Grangemouth. These merge insensibly into the lower parts of the raised beach and recent mud of the Forth.

111. Besides the level "haughs" bordering the streams, there occur abundantly over the area of the Map smaller isolated tracts of alluvium, which evidently occupy the sites of former shallow lakes in the hollows of the drift deposits. In many cases these old lake-beds have been covered with peat, which has been removed in whole or in part by agricultural operations.

112. *Peat.*—The undulating moory ground that stretches between Castlecary and the valley of the Breich Water is mantled with interrupted sheets of peat, some of which are of considerable extent, as Fauldhouse Moor, Fannyside Muir, Gardrum Moss, &c. Not a few of the peat mosses seem to occupy the sites of old lakes; in some cases, indeed, portions of the lakes still remain. The larger mosses, however, are merely fragments of what seems at one time to have been a very wide-spread covering of peat. Agricultural operations have done much to alter the face of the country in this respect within the last hundred years, but portions of the original unreclaimed mosses are still plentiful enough. Almost every hollow between the ridges to the south of Falkirk, for instance, contains its independent patch of moss. Extensive clearances have been made of the wide tracts of peat which once covered the low land of the Carse. The clays below the peat yield there a very fertile soil, hence the peat has

·been removed acre after acre, and in many cases thrown into the Forth. Lethan Moss is a large fragment of the Carse moss still unreclaimed.

113. Owing to the flatness of the ground on which some of the large peat-mosses of the central coal-fields lie the drainage is not rapid, and the spongy peat is apt to gather a large quantity of water during heavy rain. Not many years ago, after a wet season, one of the mosses in the Slamannan district swelled up and burst. The peaty mud escaped into a valley, and still covers several acres of arable land to a depth of some feet. Beneath the peat-mosses roots and trunks of large trees, principally oak and pine, are met with in abundance. The pine wood is still quite fresh and resinous, while the oak is black and decayed.

Soils.

114. The character of the soil in this as in other regions depends mainly upon that of the rock or formation lying below. By far the larger portion of the low grounds represented in the Map have boulder clay for their superficial covering, and this deposit yields as a whole a somewhat heavy tenacious soil. Unless where well drained, therefore, it is cold and wet. In some districts where it has been long under cultivation it acquires a loamy surface, from the gradual washing away by the rain of particles of clay. Considerable differences, however, may be observed in boulder clay soils, according to the materials out of which the clay has been mainly formed. For instance, where that deposit is mostly made up of the debris of Carboniferous rocks the soil becomes poor, and it regains a better quality in proportion as this debris disappears from the underlying deposit.

115. The sand and gravels of the drift series form a warm porous soil, which, however, is apt to be as undesirably light as the boulder clay soils to be stiff and retentive. Admirable soils are furnished in the Forth valley covering the 100 feet and 50 feet terraces. Those on the higher platform vary according to whether the sands or brick clays are exposed at the surface. Those at the lower level are for the most part heavy clay soils. Both these areas have the further advantage of being near the sea-level. In the bottom of the river valleys, the soil, although somewhat variable, is generally fertile, consisting in large measure of fine loam. Here and there it becomes rather sandy and light, while in other places again it passes into a heavy clay. Peat, where reclaimed, bears tolerably good crops.

116. Where the underlying rocks come bare to the surface we observe still greater diversities in the character of the soils. Thus, on the Carboniferous strata, where devoid of drift, especially on those of the Millstone Grit series, nothing but a poor hungry soil is found. Igneous rocks, on the other hand, are much more fertile. In the hollows of the basalts, where any amount of debris has accumulated, a pretty fair soil is obtained. Hence a difference may be noted between the hilly tracts in the north-west and those in the south-east quarters of the Map. In the former case, the underlying igneous rocks being sparsely coated with boulder clay, form tracts of good pasture land ; in the latter case, the sandstones, shales, and other Carboniferous strata also afford pasture, but of an inferior quality.

Economic Minerals.

117. *Building Materials.*—The chief building material in the districts included in this Map is sandstone, which is met with in each division of the Carboniferous formation, but in a workable condition, chiefly in the Limestone series, the Millstone Grit, and the Coal-measures. The Upper

Red Sandstones are quarried sparingly, as at Thornwood, near Uddingston; Brancheoch, near Cambuslang; near Bellshill, Shettleston, Langloan, &c.; but the stone, as a rule, is neither very ornamental nor very durable. Good sandstones occur in the true Coal-measures, but owing to the many faults by which the strata are traversed, the sandstones are often seamed with too many joints, and so rendered useless for building purposes. In the Clyde basin they have been very sparingly worked; the stone chiefly used in that district for ordinary purposes being the harder bands and beds that occur amongst the Upper Red Sandstone group. The sandstones of the Millstone Grit series are generally coarse-grained and soft, and are therefore not durable, and fit only for local use and unimportant structures.

118. In the northern and north-eastern districts, round Falkirk and Larbert, sandstones lying at the base of the Coal-measures are extensively worked, and from the proximity of the quarries to both railways and a canal, are both used locally and sent to a distance. Near Kilsyth sandstones on the horizon of the Highland Park or Bannockburn coal-seams are much in request; while in the Denny and Castlecary neighbourhood, the sandstones most quarried are those of the uppermost division of the Carboniferous Limestone series. All these horizons afford excellent building stone. From the great sheets of basalt near Kilsyth, curb and paving stones are extensively manufactured and sent chiefly to Glasgow, while the chips are used as road metal. In out of the way places any of the rocks of the district lying conveniently at hand are used as rubble or for dry-stone dykes; but the above are the principal sources of building material.

119. *Limestones.*—The Hurlet and Campsie Main Limestone, as well as the Hosie's seams, have long been worked extensively in the north-west part of the Map. They crop out in a great many places round Lennoxtown, and thence by Kilsyth and Denny to Stirling. They are also quarried to the north and east of Bathgate. The Calmy Limstone was formerly extensively worked, though, from the amount of sediment which it contains, it must have yielded an inferior kind of lime. The Index Limestone was extracted at Dullatur, and, though thin, was of good quality. The only limestone now worked in the central and northern districts is the Castlecary seam, which makes excellent lime both for agricultural and building purposes, and, from its comparative purity, for iron-smelting also. This seam is likewise worked at Levenseat and Standhill. Most of the limestones seem to have been formerly much sought after, as may be inferred from the numerous abandoned quarries. Since the introduction of railways into the district, however, lime from a distance can be procured better and cheaper.

120. *Road-Metal.*—The patches and dykes of igneous rocks which are represented on the Map as intersecting the Carboniferous strata, almost invariably yield excellent materials for road-metal, and they are invariably quarried for this and for rough building purposes. The contemporaneous igneous rocks of the Bathgate Hills yield rock of a similar character. The igneous rocks of the Kilsyth Hills and the Cathkin Hills also form durable road metal, but not of so excellent a quality as the intrusive and contemporaneous basalt rocks of the coal-fields and the Bathgate Hills.

121. *Fuel.*—The area occupied by coal-bearing strata is indicated on the Map. The seams consist of common, splint, gas, parrot, or cannel, and steam coal, the latter being developed chiefly in the neighbourhood of intrusive igneous rocks. No workable coals occur in the Millstone Grit, nor in that area of the Calciferous Sandstone series which comes into the present Map. *Peat* occurs some what plentifully (see par. 112), and of good quality; but, with abundant coal in the neighbourhood, it is not now used. It might be worked in the event of coal rising much in price;

but as none of the peat-mosses attains a great depth, this resource would soon be exhausted, for a large proportion of the peat indicated upon the Map is too thin and light even for domestic purposes.

122. *Oil Shales.*—The bed known as the Kiltongue Musselband is pretty extensively worked in the Clyde and North-central basins for oil, especially in the Airdrie district. It is worked also at Shotts and elsewhere. One of the most valuable seams from which oil has been obtained is the well-known Boghead or Torbanehill parrot, but it is fast approaching exhaustion.

123. *Bedded Ores.*—Two kinds of iron ore are worked, viz., *clayband* and *blackband*. In the coal-fields of the Clyde basin the principal seams of the latter have been worked for many years, and are approaching exhaustion. The various bands are the Palacecraig Ironstone, Airdrie Blackband, Newarthill or Cleland Roughband, Bellside or Greenhill Ironstone, Kiltongue Musselband, Calderbraes or Kennelburn Ironstone, Upper Slaty Ironstone, and Lower Slaty Ironstone. In the North-central basin occur the Upper and Lower Slaty Ironstones.

124. Several other bands are found in connection with coal-seams, but they are only lenticular and local, and would not pay to work separately from the coal-seam. They occur along with the Johnstone coal at Slamannan, the lower Coxroad or Balmoral coal, and the Auchingane coal. Blackband ironstone is extensively mined at Kilsyth and Denny, where several seams are found in the Carboniferous Limestone series. Clay ironstone is worked in connection with the Shotts Furnace coal and the Ball or Coalinshields coal; and two bands of clay ironstone occur in the underlying Millstone Grit series, viz., the ginstone, and the curdly or curly ironstone. Clayband ironstone of good quality used to be obtained at Banton and Denny, in the Carboniferous Limestone series. Several seams of the same mineral have been mined at Falkirk among the strata immediately overlying the slaty-band ironstone. They have also been got from the horizon of the Brighton main and Auchingane coals.

125. *Alum Shale.*—This mineral has long been largely mined in the Campsie district. It occurs there immediately below the Hurlet or main limestone as a seam of pyritous dark shale from two to fourteen feet in thickness. Exposed to the air it decomposes, and an abundant efflorescence of alum appears. Alum is also made from a shale connected with the Coxroad coal, near Falkirk, by calcining it and treating it with sulphuric acid. It is, strictly speaking, not an alum shale, though used in the manufacture of that substance.

126. *Brick Clays.*—Excellent fire-bricks are made from the fire-clays which occur among the Coal-measures, and from the Carboniferous rocks generally. In the neighbourhood of Falkirk the low part of the Coal-measures produces the greatest quantity. Fire-clays of excellent quality are also largely worked in the Millstone Grit series to the east of Glasgow.

127. In the neighbourhood of Falkirk the boulder clay is extensively ground up with some of the coarser fire-clays and shales, and makes good bricks. More usually, however, it is the layers of stratified clay lying upon that deposit, or intercalated with it, which are employed for this purpose. The latter are, on the whole, interrupted and of small extent, while the upper clays sometimes cover considerable areas, as in the 50 feet and 100 feet terraces. These terrace clays make good bricks, and at Grahamstown they are manufactured into the common kinds of earthenware.

128. *Sand.*—This useful material may be obtained in large quantities from the terraces just mentioned, from the intercalated sand-beds in the boulder-clay, or from the upper sandy and gravelly drift (see pars. 99, 100, 101).

APPENDIX TO SHEET 31.

I.—LIST OF LOCALITIES

FROM WHICH FOSSILS HAVE BEEN COLLECTED BY THE GEOLOGICAL SURVEY IN
WEST LINLITHGOW, NORTH-EAST LANARK, SOUTH-EAST STIRLINGSHIRE,
WITH DETACHED PORTION OF DUMBARTON.—(Sheet 31.)

Collectors—Messrs J. BENNIE and A. MACCONOCHIE.

*(The numbers are those by which the localities are denoted in the succeeding List
of Fossils.*

A.—Linlithgow, Bathgate, and Whitburn Districts.

1. Chance Pit, No. 21, Kinneil, near Bo'ness.
2. Mingle Pit, No. 1, Kinneil.
3. Loudon Pit, No. 18, Kinneil.
4. No. 4 Pit, Kinneil.
5. Snab Pit, 1 mile S.W. of Bo'ness.
6. Dean Pit, No. 13, Kinneil, near Bo'ness.
7. Dykeneuk Old Quarry, Kinneil, 1½ mile S.W. of Bo'ness.
8. River Avon, 100 yards below Kinneil Mill, 1 mile N.W. of Linlithgow.
9. River Avon, opposite Little Mill, 1½ mile N.W. of Linlithgow.
10. Craigenbuck Old Sandstone Quarry (from mine nearly opposite).
11. Mine on right bank of the River Avon, by railway bridge at Todd's Mill.
12. Mine below do.
13. River Avon, at railway bridge, near Avonbank, N.W. of Linlithgow.
14. Linlithgow Bridge, at Linlithgow.
15. River Avon, half-way between Avon Paper Mill and Linlithgow Bridge.
16. River Avon, under Woodcockdale House, and opposite Manuel Mill.
17. Easter Carriber Farm-house, burn under, 1½ mile S.W. of Linlithgow.
18. River Avon, bend below Canal Aqueduct, 2½ miles S.W. of do.
19. Bowden Hill Limestone Mines, S.W. of do.
20. Silvermine Quarry, North, N.E. of Bathgate.
21. Silvermine Quarry, South, do.
22. Sunnyside Quarry, Knock Farm, do.
23. Galabraes Quarry, N.E. of Bathgate.
24. Petershill Quarry, do.
25. Wardlaw Quarry, 2½ miles N.E. of Bathgate.
26. Kirkton Quarry, East, near do.
27. Kirkton Quarry, West, near do
28. Hilderston Colliery, 1½ mile N.W. of do.
29. Standhill Limestone Pit, 1¼ mile S. of do.
30. Almond River, at Blackburn.
31. Murrayfield Old Pit, shale heaps at, near Blackburn.
32. Blackburn.
33. Murrayfield Old Quarry, near Blackburn.
34. Skolieburn, S. of Blackburn; upper quarry below bridge, west of Addiewell
    workmen's houses.
35. Skolieburn, shale *in situ*, on the left bank, below bridge, as before.
36. Skolieburn, quarry-heaps on right bank, as before.

37. Skolieburn, below road at Addiebrown Hill.
38. Skolieburn, at wood near do.
39. Woodmuir Burn, at bend half-way between two roads, 2½ miles S. of Whitburn.
40. Old Coal Pit on roadside, W. of Longford, 3 miles S. of Blackburn.
41. No. 16 Mine, Addiewell, near Blackburn,
42. Levenseat Limestone Pit, near Fauldhouse.
43. Levenseat Quarry, near do.
44. Climpy Quarry, near do.
45. Whitehouse Quarry, half a mile E. of Levenseat.
46. Curly Ironstone Pits and Old Pit-heaps, Gladsmuir Hills, about 2 miles S. of Fauldhouse.
47. No. 10 Pit, Boghead (James Russell & Sons), Whiteside Farm, S.W. of Bathgate.
48. No. 2 Pit, Trees (W. Torrance & Co.), 2 miles S.W. of Bathgate.
49. Nos. 14, 15, and 16 Pits, Barbauchlaw, Armadale (Monkland Iron and Steel Co.), 2½ miles W. by S. of Bathgate.
50. No. 15 Pit, Coppers (Shotts Iron Co.), near Westfield, 3 miles S.W. of Bathgate.
51. Nos. 5 and 10 Pits, Bathville (J. Watson & Sons), Bathville Oil Works, 2½ miles S. W. of Bathgate.
52. Fauldhouse Colliery, 4½ miles S.W. of Blackburn.❘

B.—Kirk of Shotts, Airdrie, Coatbridge, Bothwell, Cambuslang, and Shettleston Districts.

53. Slatyband Pits at Crofthead, near Fauldhouse.
54. Coal Pit near Crofthead, do.
55. Slatyband Ironstone Pits at Benhar Row, 1 mile S.S.W. of Harthill.
56. Slatyband Pits, Polkemmet Moor, 1½ mile S. by E. of Harthill.
57. Pit near Hartwood Hill, 1 mile W. of Dikehead.
58. Coal Pit near Wester Baton, 1 mile N. of Dikehead.
59. Old Pit on side of burn at Dikehead.
60. Streamlet in wood, a little N.W. of Hills of Murdeston Farm, 2 miles N. of Shotts Kirk.
61. No. 1 Pit, Mount Cow, 1½ mile N.N.E. of do.
62. No. 2 Pit, Spindleside, 3½ miles do.
63. No. 1 Pit, Duntillan, at Scarknowe, 1 mile N.N.W. of do.
64. No. 3 Pit, Midge, at Bellside Railway Station, 3½ miles N.E. of do.
65. Coal Pit a little south of Fortissat, 1½ mile S.S.E. of do.
66. Pit at Manse, 1½ mile S. of do.
67. Pit on roadside at Turnpike, ½ mile west of last locality.
68. Old Coal Pit, near Auchinlea, 3 miles S.W. of Shotts Kirk.
69. No. 1 Pit, Windy Edge, 3 miles S.W. of do.
70. No. 2 New Pit, Windy Edge, side of Mineral Railway, 3 miles S.W. of do.
71. No. 3 New Pit, do., do.
71. Old Pit near Newarthill.
73. Pit on roadside near Greenhill House, E. of Newarthill.
74. Pit a little S. by W. of last locality.
75. Shotts Burn, at bridge near Langside, 1¾ mile W. of Shotts Kirk.
76. The same, 250 yards further down stream.
77. The same, below Fairybank, 2¾ miles W. of do.
78. Musselband Pit, a little N.E. of Auchinlea, near Newarthill.
79. Pit, a little N.E. of Auchinlea, near do.
80. Coal Pit, side of Mineral Railway, 2¾ miles S.W. of Shotts Kirk.
81. Old Pit at Lillyloch, 2½ miles N. by W. of do.
82. North Calder Water, 150 yards above road leading to Chapelhall, between Airdrie and Newarthill.
83. Mine on Shotts Burn, above Chapelhall Iron-Works, near Airdrie.
84. Shotts Burn, Mine at Linn, opposite Budshaw, 2¾ miles S.S.E. of do.
85. Newarthill Burn, 150 yards below road leading from Newarthill to Legbrannock, 3¾ miles S. by E. of Airdrie.
86. Coal Pit, a little to S.W. of Racecourse, do.
87. Ironstone Pit, in Racecourse, do.
88. Old Pit, at Thrushbank, 1 mile N. by E. of do.
89. Burn, at cottage near Rig, 2¾ miles N. of do.
90. Cameron Burn, in glen near Mine to "Blind Coal," opposite Auldshields, 3¼ miles N. of Airdrie.
91. Cameron Burn, a little further down stream.
92. Cameron Burn, close to road leading to Greengairs.
93. Streamlet above Caldercruix Station, 4 miles E. by N. of Airdrie.

94. Glenmavis Burn, in wood at Farm, 1 mile N. of Airdrie.
95. Glenmavis Burn, in wood, ¼ mile S. of Glenmavis.
96. Old Pit, near Delmacouther, 1¼ mile N. by E. of Airdrie.
97. Coal Pit at Airdriehill Farm, near do.
98. Ironstone Pit, side of Railway, 1¼ mile S.W. of Langridge-End, near do.
99. Old Coal Pit, do., do.
100. B.B. Ironstone Pit, at Darngavel, 2½ miles N. by E. of Airdrie.
101. Old Oil Shale Works, a little W. of do.
102. Pit at Palacecraig, near do.
103. Old Ironstone Pit near Palacecraig.
104. No. 10 Pit Carnbroe, 2½ miles S.S.W. of Airdrie.
105. Ironstone Pit, ½ mile E. of Palacecraig.
106. Pit near Palacecraig, near Airdrie.
107. Coal Pit, Todholes, a little W. of Calder Iron-Works, near do.
108. Bedlay Railway Cutting, ½ mile E. of Chryston, near Coatbridge.
109. Old Pit at side of stream, near Glenpark Cottage, ½ mile E. of Mollinburn, near Coatbridge.
109a. Limestone Pits, ½ mile S. of Mollinburn, 3½ miles N. of do.
110. Glenboig Brick-Works, 2¼ miles N. of do.
111. Coal Pit, at Heatheryknowe House, 2 miles W. of do.
112. New Coal Pit, 250 yards from Uddingston, near Bothwell.
113. River Clyde, at Craighead House, near do.
114. Pit near Carmyle, 1 mile N. of Cambuslang.
115. Coal Pit, at Great Newlands, 1¼ mile S.E. of Baillieston.
116. North Calder Water, above Bredisholm, 1½ mile E.S.E. of do.
117. Pit on roadside at Nackerty, 1¾ mile S.E. of do.
118. Coal Pit, at Rosebank, 1¾ mile E. of do.
119. New Pit, ½ mile E. of do.
120. Garnkirk Brick-Works, 3½ miles N. of do.
120a. Coal Pit at Mount Vernon Station, 1 mile S.W. of do.
121. Old Pit at Shettleston.
122. Pit at West Hills, Shettleston.
123. Railway Cutting at Toll, 1 mile N.E. of Glasgow.
124. Old Pit, S.E. of Kennyhill, 1½ mile N.E. of Glasgow.
125. Old Shank to Fireclay, south side of Canal, near Blackhill Lochs, 1½ mile N.N.E. of do.
126. Quarry, N. of Germiston Mains, 1½ mile W. of Hogganfield Loch.
127. Ironstone Pit, N.E. of Balornock House, 1½ mile W. of Hogganfield.
128. Old Quarries, N.E. of Barnulloch, N.W. of do.
129. Old Quarries at Robroyston House, N. by W. of do.
130. Old Quarry at Woodhill, near Auchencairn, N. by W. of do.

C. Kirkintilloch, Lennoxtown, Kilsyth, and Cumbernauld Districts.

131. Railway Cutting near Myremailing, 2¾ miles S.W. of Kirkintilloch.
132. Old Pit, N. of Loch Farm, 1½ miles S. by W. of do.
132. New Pit, at Waterside, 1½ miles E.S.E. of do.
134. Luggie Water, at Waterside, do.
135. Glenwhapple Burn, a little S. of Craigenglen, 1½ miles S. of Lennoxtown.
136. Glenwhapple Burn, a little N. of do. do.
137. Ironstone Pit, W. of Muirhead, 1½ miles S.W. of do.
138. Culloch Slap Mine, 1 mile W.S.W. of Lennoxtown.
139. Boyd's Burn Mine, near Lennoxtown.
140. Burn a little below Bencloich Mill, N.E of Lennoxtown.
141. Burn passing Bencloich Mill, above wall forming limit of cultivated ground, N.E. of Lennoxtown.
142. Mine, a little north of Glorat House, 1 mile N. E. of Lennoxtown.
143. Mine to Main Limestone, N. of Balgrochan, near Lennoxtown.
144. Burn Rannie, at Balgrochan, near Lennoxtown.
145. Limeworks at Scullingour, 1 mile N. of Lennoxtown.
146. Old Quarries along foot of Campsie Hills, N.E. of Lennox town.
147. Junction of Burniebrae and Spouthead Burns, 1 mile N. of Milton of Campsie.
148. Glenwhapple Burn, north of Craigenglen, near Lennoxtown.
149. Cowie's Glen, Burniebrae Burn, near Lennoxtown.
150. Most easterly branch of Spouthead Burn, 1 mile N. of Milton of Campsie.
151. Second branch of Spouthead Burn, near junction with trap, 1 mile N. of Milton of Campsie.
152. Redcleugh Burn, Spouthead Burn, at junction with the trap of the hill, 1 mile N. of Milton of Campsie.

153. Burniebrae Burn, close to junction with the trap of the hill, 1¼ mile N.E. of Milton of Campsie.
154. Burniebrae Burn, about half way between trap and wall, 1¼ mile N.E. of Milton of Campsie.
155. Burniebrae Burn, further down burn, below wall, 1¼ mile N.E. of Milton of Campsie.
156. Burniebrae Burn, still further down burn, at road, 1¼ mile N.E. of Milton of Campsie.
157. Burniebrae Burn, east of Shield's Cottage, near Milton of Campsie.
158. Old Quarry, west by Drumairn, 1¼ mile N.E. of Milton of Campsie.
159. Corrieburn, at stone wall on hillside above Cairnbog Farm, 2¼ miles W.N.W. of Kilsyth.
160. Corrieburn, at side of glen, below stone wall, 2¼ miles W.N.W. of Kilsyth.
161. Corrieburn, large escarpment in most easterly branch of, 2 miles W.N.W. of Kilsyth.
162. Burn, half a mile N.E. of Corrie Farm, 2½ miles W.N.W. of Kilsyth.
163. Burn, at wood north of Cairnbog, 2 miles W.N.W. of Kilsyth.
164. Coal and Ironstone Pits at Bord, 2¼ miles S. by W. of Kilsyth.
165. Burn, side of railway near Westerwood, 3 miles E. of Kilsyth.
166. Old Refuse Heaps at Mines, side of Railway, 2½ miles E. of Kilsyth.
167. Old Quarry near Dullatur, 2 miles E.S.E. of Kilsyth.
168. Coal and Ironstone Pits at Solsgirth, 1½ mile E. of Kirkintilloch.
169. Garrel Burn, in glen above Kilsyth.
170. Garrel Burn, above Allanfauld.
171. Burn, a little north of Low Banton, 2½ miles E.N.E. of Kilsyth.
172. Burn, below Drumressie, 2¼ miles E.N.E. of Kilsyth.
173. Old Mine near Tomfin, 3 miles N.E. of Kilsyth.
174. Craigdouffie, small burn a little below, 3 miles N.E. of Kilsyth.
175. Old Quarry at head of stream, E. of Brockieside, 1¾ mile N. by E. of Kilsyth.
176. Castlecary Limeworks, Castlecary, near Cumbernauld.
177. Fireclay Workings, side of Railway, E. of Cumbernauld House.
178. Old Lime Workings, Cumbernauld House Policies.
179. Mouth of Old Mine, side of Railway, ¾ mile E.S.E. of Cumbernauld.
180. Small Glen at Carnbrain Farm, S. of Cumbernauld.
181. Old Quarries at Ravenswood, 1½ mile S. by W. of Cumbernauld.
182. Ravenswood Sandstone Quarry, 1½ mile S. by W. of Cumbernauld.
183. Glen, south of West Forest, 1½ mile S. of Cumbernauld.
183. Luggie Water, above Lenzie Mill, 2 miles S. of Cumbernauld.

D.—Denny, Larbert, Falkirk, Polmont, and Slamannan Districts.

184. Steel Colliery, west of Haggs, 3 miles S.S.W. of Denny.
185. Linns, near head of stream at, 3 miles W. of Denny.
186. Castle Rankine Burn, near Glenhead, 2½ miles S.W. of Denny.
187. Castle Rankine Glen, nearly opposite Castle Rankine, 1½ mile W.S.W. of Denny.
188. Old Pit, Banknock, 2 miles S.S.W. of Denny.
189. Coal Pit at Dennyloanhead, S. of Denny.
190. Pit, north of Banknock House, 2½ miles S.S.W. of Denny.
191. River Carron, above Mill, 1¼ mile W. of Denny.
192. River Carron, at Mill, 1¼ mile W. of Denny.
193. River Carron, 1 mile W. of Denny.
194. Old Quarry in wood, E. of Northfield, 2 miles N. of Denny.
195. Burn, below Mill, 1¼ mile N. of Denny.
196. Streamlet in wood, near Dogrulleck, 1 mile E.N.E. of Dunipace.
197. Ironstone Pit, N.E of Quarter House, N. of Dunipace.
198. Torburn, at crossing of Roman Road, 2½ miles N. by W. of Larbert.
199. Torburn, at Turnpike road, 2½ miles N. by W. of Larbert.
200. River Carron, cliff near Printwork, Denny.
201. Pits, N. of Carron, near Larbert.
202. Pit near Drum, 2½ miles N. of Larbert.
203. Earl of Zetland Brick and Tile Works, at Lock No. 3, Forth and Clyde Canal, near Grangemouth.
204. Old Quarry at bridge, Railway Station, Falkirk.
205. Burn near Crosshill, 2¼ miles S.S.E. of Falkirk.
206. Burn near Redding Farm, S.E. of Falkirk.
207. California, pits and sections near, 2¼ miles S.S.E. of Falkirk.
208. West Quarter Burn, nearly opposite Knowehead, 1½ mile S.E. of Falkirk.
209. Railway cutting near Redding, 2 miles E.S.E. of Falkirk.
210. Cleugh Glen, 1½ mile S. of Falkirk.

211. Small Burn, a few yards above Union Canal, 1½ mile S. E. of Falkirk.
212. Small Burn, at fault near Easter Pirley Hill, near Falkirk.
213. Small Burn, at old coal pit, further up burn.
214. Small Burn, still further up burn, at Wester Pirley Hill.
215. Small Burn, below and above road, ½ mile E. of Polmont.
216. Burn, above road, E. of Blairlodge, 1 mile S. by W. of Polmont.
217. Sandstone Quarry at Brighton, ¾ mile S. of Polmont.
218. Burn above Rumford, 1¼ mile S. of Polmont.
219. South Bantaskine, line of old quarries at, 1 mile S.S.W. of Falkirk.
220. Streamlet, north of Auchengane, 2½ miles S.W. of Falkirk.
221. Streamlet, in wood, above Railway, 3 miles W. of Falkirk.
222. Old Mine, side of canal, at Greenbank, 1½ mile W.S.W. of Falkirk.
223. Coal Pits near New Craig, 3½ miles S.S.W. of Falkirk.
224. Coal Pit, a little south of High Stanerig, 1 mile N. by W. of Falkirk.
225. Old Pit, side of Slamannan Railway, 1 mile E. of Slamannan.
226. Old Pit, E. of Anchengane, 2½ miles S.S.W. of Falkirk.
227. Barn, at road, near Glencoig House, 2 miles E. of Slamannan.
228. Coal Pit, at Blackbraes, 3 miles S. by E. of Falkirk.
229. Burn, opposite Fen Hill, 1½ mile S. of Slamannan.
230. Pits near Little Blackloch, 2 miles S. of Slamannan.
231. Pits near Blackloch, 2 miles S. of Slamannan.

II.—LIST OF FOSSILS.

Carboniferous.

Lower Carboniferous or Calciferous Sandstone Series.

CEMENT STONE GROUP.

Shale above Sandstone.

Class, etc.	Name.	Locality Number
Plantæ,	Cyclopteris.—*Sp.*	169.
	Lepidodendron (fragments),	170.
	Sphenopteris (like " Wardie Shale."—*Sp.*),	} 169.
	Stigmaria,	
Brachiopoda,	Lingula.—*Sp.*	
Pelecypoda,	Anthracomya Scotica.—*Eth. jun.?*	170.

Carboniferous Limestone Series.

LOWER LIMESTONE GROUP.

Ashy Shale above " Eurypterus " Limestone, below Main Limestone (Bathgate).

Plantæ,	Plant remains plentiful, comprising Lepidodendron, Sphenopteris, &c.	} 26.

Kirkton Marine Limestone, below Main Limestone (Bathgate).

Actinozoa,	Lonsdaleia floriformis.—*Martin?*	
Polyzoa,	Fenestella.—*Sp.*	
Brachiopoda,	Lingula mytiloides.—*Sow.*	} 27.
	Productus semireticulatus.—*Martin*,	
	Spirifera duplicicosta, *var.* crassa,	

Shale above Kirkton Marine Limestone.

Brachiopoda,	Productus semireticulatus.—*Martin*,	} 27.
	„ „ var. Martini.—*Sow.*	

Dark Shale and Nodules, a few feet under an Impure Limestone, below Main Limestone.

Class, etc.	Name.	Locality Number.
Brachiopoda,	Athyris ambigua.—*Sow.*	
	Discina nitida.—*Phillips*,	
	Orthis Michelini.—*Léveillé*,	
	,, resupinata.—*Martin*,	
	Productus longispinus.—*Sowerby*,	} 144.
	,, semireticulatus.—*Martin*,	
	,, var. Martini.—*Sow.*	
Pelecypoda,	Aviculopecten.—*Sp.*	
	Myalina sublamellosa.—*Eth. jun.* ?	
	Pteronites persulcatus.—*M'Coy*,	
Gasteropoda,	Bellerophon Urei.—*Fleming*,	

Shale over the Impure Limestone just mentioned.

Brachiopoda,	Chonetes Laguessiana.—*De Koninck*,	
	Spirifera trigonalia.—*Martin*, var.	} 144.
	Entolium Sowerbii.—*M'Coy*,	

Impure Clay-band Ironstone, below Main Limestone.

Annelida,	Serpulites.—*Sp.*	
Brachiopoda,	Chonetes Laguessiana.—*De Koninck*,	
	Productus semireticulatus.—*Martin*,	
	Rhynchonella pleurodon.—*Phillips*,	} 136.
	Aviculopecten dissimilis.—*Fleming*,	
	Entolium Sowerbii.—*M'Coy*,	
	Modiola lithodomoides.—*Eth. jun.*	

Thin Ferruginous Limestone in shale below Main Limestone.

Actinozoa,	Lithostrotion irregulare.—*Con. and Phill.* ?	
	Heterophylla Lyelli.—*Duncan*,	} 135.
	Fenestella.—*Sp.*	
Brachiopoda,	Chonetes Buchiana.—*De Koninck*,	
	Lingula mytiloides.—*Sow.*	136.
	Productus giganteus.—*Martin*,	135, 136.
	,, punctatus.—*Martin*,	135, 136.
	,, scabriculus.—*Martin*,	
	,, semireticulatus.—*Martin*,	
	Spirifera trigonalis, var. bisulcata.—*Sow.*	} 135.
	Aviculopecten interstitialis.—*Phill.*	
	,, subconoideus.—*Eth. jun.*	
	Entolium Sowerbii.—*M'Coy*,	136.
	Bellerophon Urei.—*Fleming*,	135.
	Loxonema scalaroidea.—*Phillips* ?	136.
	Megalichthys (scales, &c.),	135.

"Alum Shale" under Main Limestone.

Plantæ,	Lepidostrobus—*Sp.*	139.
Brachiopoda,	Lingula squamiformis.—*Phillips*,	138, 139.
	Spirifera Urei.—*Fleming*,	138.
Pelecypoda,	Leptodomus costellatus.—*M'Coy*,	138, 139.
	Myalina.—*Sp.*	138.
	Posidonomya corrugata.—*Etheridge*, var.	139.
	Pteronites.—*Sp.*	} 128.
Gasteropoda,	Bellerophon Urei.—*Fleming*,	

Shales and Nodules below Main Limestone.

Foraminifera,	Endothyra globolus.—*Eichwald*,	23.
Spongida, etc.	Saccammina Carteri.—*Brady*?	23.
	Stacheia polytrematoides.—*Brady*,	148.
	Valvulina decurrens.—*Brady*,	
	,, palæotrochus.—*Ehrenberg*,	} 23.
	,, ,, var. compressa,	

Class, etc.	Name.	Locality Number.
Spongida, etc.,	Palæocóryne.—*Sp.*	148.
	Hyalonema paralléla.—*M'Coy,*	23, 24.
Actinozoa,	Chætetes.—*Sp.*	
	Clisiophyllum coniseptum.—*M. Edw.*	⎫
	Cyclophyllum fungites.—*Fleming,*	⎬ 23.
	Dibunophyllum ?—*Sp.*	⎭
	Heterophylla Lyelli.—*Duncan,*	248.
	Lithostrotion junceum.—*Fleming,*	23.
	Lonsdaleia.—*Sp.*	23.
	Zaphrentis Cliffordana.—*Ed. and H. ?*	23.
Echinodermata,	Archæocidaris Urei.—*Fleming* (spines, &c.),	142, 148.
Annelida,	Serpulites carbonarius.—*M'Coy,*	23, 24, 145, 148.
	Spirorbis caperatus.—*M'Coy,*	23.
	,, (near S. globosus, *M'Coy*),	148.
Crustacea,	Bairdia curta.—*M'Coy,*	⎫
	,, elongata.—*Münster,*	⎪
	,, grandis.—*J. and K.,*	⎬ 23.
	,, Hisingeri.—*Münster,*	⎪
	,, plebeia.—*Reuss,*	⎭
	Dithyrocaris (fragment).—*Sp.*	145.
	Kirkbya Permiana.—*Jones,*	⎱ 23.
	Leperditia Okeni.—*Münster,*	⎰
Polyzoa,	Fenestella.—*Sp.*	148.
	Glauconome.—*Sp.*	148.
	Diastopora megastoma.—*M'Coy,*	23.
	Rhabdomeson gracile.—*Phillips,*	148.
	,, *Sp.*	23, 24.
Brachiopoda,	Athyris ambigua.—*Sow.*	23.
	Athyris Roysii.—*Léveillé,*	23.
	Chonetes Laguessiana.—*De Koninck,*	23.
	Discina nitida.—*Phillips,*	45.
	Lingula mytiloides.—*Sow.*	136.
	,, squamiformis.—*Phill.*	140, 142.
	Productus aculeatus.—*Martin,*	38.
	,, cora.—*D'Orbigny ?*	140.
	,, latissimus.—*Sow. ?*	136.
	,, longispinus.—*Sow.*	23, 145.
	,, punctatus.—*Martin,*	23, 136.
	,, semireticulatus.—*Martin,*	23, 136.
	,, ,, var. pugilis.—*Phill.*	236.
	,, spinulosus.—*Sow.*	23.
	Spirifera duplicicosta.—*Phill.*	136.
	,, trigonalis.—*Martin, var.*	136.
	,, Urei.—*Fleming,*	145, 136, 140.
	Strophomena analoga.—*Phillips,*	143.
	Terebratula sacculus.—*Martin, var.*	136.
Pelecypoda,	Aviculopecten dissimilis.—*Fleming,*	23, 24, 136, 140.
	,, interstitialis.—*Phillips,*	145.
	Entolium Sowerbii.—*M'Coy,*	140.
	Leptodomus costellatus.—*M'Coy,*	140, 143, 146.
	Nucula brevirostris.—*Phillips,*	140.
	,, gibbosa.—*Fleming,*	136, 140.
	,, Youngi.—*Etheridge, jun. ?*	148.
Gasteropoda,	Bellerophon decussatus.—*Fleming,*	148.
	,, Urei.—*Fleming,*	140, 145, 146.
	Loxonema rugifera.—*Phillips,*	136, 148.
	Murchisonia striatula.—*De Koninck ?*	148.
	Natica variata.—*Phillips ?*	148.
	Polyphemopsis fusiformis.—*Sow. ?*	148.
	Trochus brevirostris.—*Phill. ?*	148.
Cephalopoda,	Discites quadratus.—*Fleming ?*	145.
Pisces,	Elonichthys striolatus.—*Ag.* (scales),	148.
	Megalichthys (scales),	148.
	Petalodus Hastingsii.—*Owen,*	24.
	,, lobatus.—*Etheridge, jun.*	23.

E

Shale and Wild-Parrot Coal, 18 in. to 24 in. below Main or Hurlet
Limestone, and above "Hurlet" Coal.

Class, etc.	Name.	Locality Number.
Echinodermata,	Archæocidaris.—(? *n. Sp.* spines),	
Annelida,	Serpulites carbonarius.—*M'Coy;*	
	Lingula.—*Sp.*	
	Productus longispinus.—*Sow.*	
	Orthotetes crenistria.—*Phillips,*	
	Aviculopecten ornatus.—*Etheridge, jun.*	41.
	Entolium Sowerbii.—*M'Coy,*	
	Leptodomus costellatus.—*M'Coy;*	
	Pteronites persulcatus.—*M'Coy,*	
	Solemya primæva.—*Phillips,*	
Gasteropoda,	Bellerophon Urei.—*Fleming,*	

Hurlet, Main, Bathgate, or No. 1 Limestone.

Foraminifera, etc.,	Valvulina palæotrochus.—*Ehrenberg,*	22.
	Hyalonema parallela.—*M'Coy,*	24.
Actinozoa,	Cyclophyllum fungites.—*Fleming,*	20?, 24.
	Lithostrotion junceum.—*Fleming,*	21, 24,
	Lonsdalcia floriformis.—*Martin ?*	22, 23, 24.
	Rhodophyllum ?—*Sp.*	20.
Echinodermata,	Archæocidaris Urei.—*Fleming* (spines, &c.),	24.
Crustacea,	Griffithides.—*Sp.*	23.
Brachiopoda,	Orthotetes crenistria.—*Phillips,*	162, 23, 24.
	Productus aculeatus.—*Martin,*	23, 24, 162.
	„ giganteus.—*Martin,*	22, 24 ?
	,, longispinus.—*Sow.*	24, 140, 162, 174.
	,, punctatus.—*Martin,*	24.
	,, scabriculus.—*Martin,*	24, 140.
	,, semireticulatus.—*Martin,*	23, 24.
	,, ,, var. pugilis,	140.
	,, ,, var. concinnus,	24.
	,, spinulosus.—*Sow.*	24.
	Spirifera duplicicosta.—*Phill.*	24.
	„ glabra.—*Martin ?*	174.
	,, trigonalis.—*Martin, var.*	162.
	Terebratula sacculus, var. hastata.—*Sow.*	24.
	Strophomena analoga.—*Phillips,*	140.
Pelecypoda,	Aviculopecten interstitialis.—*Phillips,*	174.
	,, sublobatus.—*Phillips ?*	174.
	Modiola lithodomoides.—*Eth. jun.*	162.
	Pinna flabelliformis.—*Martin,*	23.
Cephalopoda,	Orthoceras sulcatum.—*Fleming,*	174.
Pisces,	Xystrodus striatus.—*Agassiz,*	24.

Calcareous Band of Shale in the Main or Hurlet Limestone.

Crustacea,	Griffithides mesotuberculatus.—*M'Coy,*	
	Discina nitida.—*Phillips,*	
	Productus aculeatus.—*Martin,*	
	„ punctatus.—*Martin,*	159.
	,, scabriculus.—*Martin,*	
	Spiriferina laminosa.—*M'Coy ?*	
	Aviculopecten sabanisotus.—*Sp. nov.?*	

Calcareous Shales resting on Main or Hurlet Limes.

Actinozoa,	Lithostrotion cæspitosum.—*M'Coy ?*	
	„ junceum.—*Fleming,*	160.
	Zaphrentis Enniskillini.—*Ed. & H.*	
Echinodermata,	Archæocidaris (spines, plates, &c.),	160.
Annelida,	Spirorbis (near S. globosus.—*M'Coy*),	161.
	„ Sp.	160.
	Ortonia carbonaria.—*Young,*	161.

Class, etc.	Name.	Locality Number
Crustacea,	Griffithides mesotuberculatus.—*M'Coy,*	146.
Polyzoa,	Rhabdomeson, *Sp.* ; and Sulcoretepora.—*Sp.*	161.
Brachiópóda,	Athyris ambigua.—*Sow.*	160.
	,, Roysii.—*Léveillé,*	146, 160.
	Chonetes Laguessiana.—*De Kon.*	146, 160.
	,, polita.—*M'Coy,*	161.
	Orthis Michelini.—*Léveillé,*	160.
	,, resupinata.—*Martin,*	160.
	Orthotetes crenistria.—*Phillips,*	160.
	Productus aculeatus.—*Martin,*	160.
	,, longispinus.—*Sow.*	146, 160.
	,, punctatus.—*Martin,*	160.
	,, scabriculus.—*Martin,*	160.
	,, semireticulatus, *var.* pugilis.—*Phill.*	160.
	,, spinulosus.—*Sow.*	160.
	Rhynchonella pleurodon.—*Phill.*	160.
	Spirifera duplicicosta.—*Phill. ?*	160.
	,, ovalis.—*Phill.*	160.
	Spiriferina cristata.—*Schlotheim,*	160.
Pelecypoda,	Aviculopecten dissimilis.—*Flem.*	
	,, tesselatus.—*Phill.*	
	Pinna.—*Sp.*	} 160.
	Pteronites persulcatus.—*M'Coy,*	
Pisces,	Megalichthys (scales),	
	Petalodus (fragment),	

Shale above Main, Hurlet, or Bathgate Limestone.

Actinozoa,	Zaphrentis Cliffordana.—*Ed. & H.*	20.
	,, Delanoui.—*Ed. & H.*	20.
Echinodermata,	Archæocidaris (spines, &c.),	146.
	Poteriocrinus crassus.—*Miller,*	23.
Crustacea,	Bairdia ampla.—*Reuss,*	20.
	,, elongata.—*Münster,*	20.
	,, grandis.—*J. & K.*	20.
	,, Hisingeri.—*Münster,*	23.
	,, plebeia.—*Reuss,*	23.
	Kirkbya Permiana.—*Jones,*	20, 23.
	,, ,, ,, var.	20.
	Primitia Scotica.—*Jones,*	20.
Brachiopoda,	Athyris ambigua.—*Sow.*	20, 21, 23
	Discina nitida.—*Phillips,*	20.
	Lingula squamiformis.—*Phill.*	146.
	Orthis resupinata.—*Martin ?*	20.
	Rhynchonella pleurodon.—*Phill.*	20, 21
	Terebratula sacculus.—*Martin,*	21.
Pelecypoda,	Aviculopecten dissimilis.—*Flem.*	146.
	,, papyraceus.—*Sow. ?*	146.
	Conocardium.—*Sp.*	146.
	Modiola lithodomoides—*Eth. jun.*	146.
Cephalopoda,	Discites quadratus.—*Fleming,*	146.
Pisces,	Xystrodus striatus,	20.

Shale below Hosie Limestone.

Plantæ,	Lepidodendron.—*Sp.*	
Actinozoa,	Zaphrentis Enniskillini.—*Ed. & H.*	
Brachiópóda,	Orthis resupinata.—*Martin,*	} 30.
	Productus longispinus.—*Sow.*	
	Spirifera trigonalis.—*Martin,*	

Clay-Band Ironstone, a few feet below Hosie.

Pisces,	Megalichthys (scales and teeth),	} 137.
	Rhizodopsis (scales),	

Bituminous Shale under Hosie Limestone.

Pisces,	Elonichthys (scales, &c.),	141

Altered Shale between Hosie Limestone and "Lake Stone" Trap Rock.

Class, etc.	Name.	Locality Number.
Brachiopoda, .	. Productus scabriculus.—*Martin ?*	.
	Spirifera trigonalis, *var.* bisulcata.—*Sow.*	.
Pelecypoda,	. Aviculopecten subanisotus.—*Sp. nov ?.*	.
	Pinna flabelliformis —*Martin,*	.
	Edmondia unioniformis.—*Phillips,*	. 34.
	Entolium Sowerbii.—*M'Coy,*	.
	Myalina.—*Sp.*	.
	Pleurophorus ?—*Sp.*	.
	Undetermined bivalve (very common),	.

Hosie Limestone.

Echinodermata,	. Archæocidaris (spines, &c.),	. . 141.
Crustacea,	. Griffithides mucronatus.—*M'Coy,*	. . 141.
Brachiopoda, .	. Athyris ambigua.—*Sow.*	. . 194.
	Rhynchonella pleurodon.—*Phillips ?*	. 185.
Pelecypoda, .	. Aviculopecten interstitialis.—*Phillips,*	. 185.
	Nucula gibbosa.—*Fleming,* .	. 185, 194.
Gasteropoda	. Bellerophon decussatus.—*Fleming,*	. 185,
	Dentalium ingens.—*De Kon. ?*	. . 185.

Shales and Nodules above Hosie Limestone.

Foraminifcra, &c.,	. Trochammina incerta.—*D'Orb.* .	. . 31.
	Palæacis cyclostoma.—*Phillips,* .	. 31.
Actinozoa	. Lithostrotion (L. irregulare, or L. cæspitosum ?), .	. 25.
	Syringopora.—*Sp.*	. 25.
	Chætetes tumidus.—*Phillips ?*	. 192.
Echinodermata,	. Archæocidaris (spines, &c.),	. 31, 35.
Annelida,	. Serpulites carbonarius.—*M'Coy,* .	. 25.
Crustacea,	. Griffithides mesotuberculatus.—*M'Coy,*	. 34, 37.
	,, mucronata.—*M'Coy,* .	. 34 175.
Polyzoa, .	. Fenestella.—*Sp.* .	. 25, 37.
	,, (near F. bicellulata.—*Eth. jun.*),	. 34.
	Synocladia carbonaria.—*Eth. jun.*	. 34.
Brachiopoda, .	. Discina nitida.—*Phillips,* .	. { 36, 37, 141, 193 ?
	Lingula mytiloides.—*Sow.* .	. { 31, 36 ?, 37, 157, 175,
	,, squamiformis.—*Phillips,*	. 36, 141.
	Orthis Michelini.—*Léveillé,*	. 35.
	,, resupinata.—*Martin,*	. { 25, 34, 36, 37, 141.
	Orthotetes crenistria.—*Phillips,* .	. 25, 37.
	Chonetes Laguessiana.—*De Kon.*	. 31.
	Productus longispinus.—*Sow.*	. { 25, 31, 34, 35, 36, 37.
	,, punctatus.—*Martin,* .	. 25.
	,, scabriculus.—*Martin?* .	. 34.
	,, semireticulatus.—*Martin,*	. 25 ?, 31, 34.
	Rhynchonella pleurodon.—*Phillips,*	. 34, 36, 192.
	Spirifera lineata.—*Martin ?*	. 34.
	,, trigonalis.—*Martin,* var.	. 34.
	,, Urei.—*Fleming,*	. { 31, 33, 35 ?, 141, 175,
	Spiriferina cristata.—*Schlotheim,*	. 25, 36.
Pelecypoda,	. Aviculopecten dissimilis.—*Fleming,*	. 25, 34.
	Leptodomus costellatus.—*M'Coy,*	. 38, 172.
	Modiola lithodomoides.—*Eth. jun.*	. 25, 37.
	Nucula brevirostris.—*Phillips,*	. 31.
	,, gibbosa.—*Fleming,*	. 31, 172, 193.
	Nuculana attenuata.—*Fleming,*	. 31, 175.
	Pinna flabelliformis.—*Martin,*	. 25, 35, 36.
	Posidonomya corrugata.—*Etheridge,*	. { 141, 150?, 172, 175, 191 ?
	Sanguinolites (near S. transversus.—*Portloc*),	37
	Solenomya primæva.—*Phillips,*	. 19.

Class, etc.	Name.	Locality Number.
Gasteropoda,	Bellerophon decussatus.—*Fleming*,	31, 36, 191.
	„ „ var. striatus,	33.
	„ Oldhami.—*Portlock*,	33.
	„ Urei.—*Fleming*,	{ 31, 34, 37, 172, 191 ?, 193.
	Euomphalus carbonarius.—*Sow.*	31, 141, 175.
	Macrocheilus.—*Sp.*	36.
Pteropoda,	Conularia quadrisulcata.—*Sow.*	192, 193.
Cephalopoda,	Actinoceras giganteum.—*Sow. ?*	141.
	Goniatites.—*Sp.*	31, 141.

Beds of L. Limestone Group of doubtful position.—Coarse Arenaceous Limestone (below Main?).

Annelida,	Serpulites,	152.
Brachiopoda,	Athyris ambigua.—*Sow.*	152.
	Discina nitida.—*Phillips*,	152.
	Camarophoria crumena.—*Martin*,	151.
	Orthotetes crenistria.—*Phillips*,	152.
	Productus aculeatus.—*Martin*,	151, 152.
	„ costatus.—*Sow.*	151.
	„ longispinus.—*Sow.*	152.
	„ semireticulatus.—*Martin*,	151, 152.
Pelecypoda,	Edmondia sulcata.—*Fleming*,	151.
	Pteronites.—*Sp.*	152.
Gasteropoda,	Bellerophon Urei.—*Fleming*,	151.

Thin Ferruginous Band under last-named Bed.

Brachiopoda,	Camarophoria.—*Sp.*	
	Productus semireticulatus.—*Martin*,	
Pelecypoda,	Aviculopecten ornatus.—*Eth. jun.*	} 153.
	„ subconoideus.—*Eth. jun.*	
	Edmondia unioniformis.—*Phillips*,	
	Nuculana attenuata.—*Fleming*,	
	Sanguinolites triscostatus.—*Portlock ?*	
Gasteropoda,	Bellerophon decussatus.—*Fleming*,	} 153.
	„ Urei.—*Fleming.*	

Shale in connection with last-named Bed.

Plantæ,	Sphenopteris.—2 *Sps.*	154.
Foraminifera,	Stacheia.—*Sp.*	
Echinodermata,	Archæocidaris (spines, plates, &c.),	} 151.
Annelida,	Ortonia carbonaria.—*Young*,	
Crustacea,	Eurypterus (fragment with ornamentation),	154.
Brachiopoda,	Chonetes polita.—*M'Coy*,	
	Discina nitida.—*Phillips*,	
	Lingula squamiformis.—*Phillips*,	
	Strophomena analoga.—*Phillips*,	} 151.
Pelecypoda,	Entolium Sowerbii.—*M'Coy*,	
	Nucula gibbosa.—*Fleming*,	
	Pteronites persulcatus.—*M'Coy*,	

MIDDLE LIMESTONE GROUP, OR EDGE-COAL SERIES.

(L. Coal Measures of some writers.)

Shale above the "Brown Stone" portion of the Bo'ness Lower Ironstone.

Pelecypoda,	Anthracoptera tumida.—*Sp. nov.*	2, 3.

Sandstone in Bo'ness Main Coal.

Plantæ,	Lepidodendron.—*Sp.*	28.

Bo'ness Upper Ironstone.

Class, etc.	Name.	Locality Number.
Plantœ,	Lepidostrobus (long, thin form),	5.
Annelida,	Spirorbis.—*Sp.*	4.
Pelecypoda,	Anthracomya (crushed examples),	5.
Pisces,	Cœlacanthus lepturus.—*Ag.* (scales),	4.
	Eurynotus.—*Sp.* (scales),	4.
	Megalichthys (scales, and other remains),	6.
	Rhizodopsis, ,, ,,	6.

Roof of Splint Coal.

Brachiopoda,	Discina nitida.—*Phillips?*	5.
	Lingula mytiloides.—*Sow?*	5, 6.
	,, squamiformis.—*Phillips,*	5, 6.
Pisces,	Eurynotus.—*Sp.* (scales, &c.),	5, 6.
	Fissodus Pattoni.—*Eth. jun.*	6.
	Megalichthys.—*Sp.* (scales, remains, &c.),	5, 6.
	Pœcilodus.—*Sp.* (single teeth),	5, 6.
	Rhizodopsis (scales and remains),	5, 6.
	Rhizodus.—*Sp.* (scales),	6.

Shale, roof of Smithy Coal.

Echinodermata,	Archæocidaris? (teeth),	1.
Brachiopoda,	Lingula squamiformis.—*Phillips,*	1, 3.
	Productus (dorsal valves),	1, 3.
Pelecypoda,	Aviculopecten (near A. planicostatus.—*M'Coy*),	1.
	Leptodomus costellatus.—*M'Coy,*	1.
	Myalina.—(small *n. Sp?*)	1.
	Nucula.—*N. Sp?* (near N. lævirostrum.—	
	Portlock),	1.
	Pteronites.—*Sp.*	1.
	Schizodus.—(*Sp.* near S. centralis.—*M'Coy*),	1.
	Solenopsis.—(*Sp.* near S. minor.—*M'Coy*),	1.
Gasteropoda,	Bellerophon Urei.—*Fleming,*	1.
	Murchisionia striatula.—*De Koninck?*	1.
Pisces.	Hybodus? (spine).	1.
	Strepsodus sauroides (teeth),	1.

UPPER LIMESTONE GROUP.

Index, Cowglen, or Rough Limestone.

Brachiopoda,	Athyris ambigua.—*Sow.*	
	Productus latissimus.—*Sow.*	
	,, giganteus.—*Martin,*	} 167.
Pelecypoda,	Edmondia sulcata.—*Fleming,*	
Pisces,	Xystrodus striatus.—*Agassiz,*	

Shale over the Index or Cowglen Limestone.

Crustacea.	Griffithides mesotuberculatus.—*M'Coy,*	167.
Brachiopoda,	Lingula squamiformis.—*Phill?*	133, 167.
Pelecypoda,	Nuculana intermedia.—*Eth. jan.*	167.
	Posidonomya corrugata.—*Etheridge,*	133.
Gasteropoda,	Bellerophon Urei.—*Fleming,*	167.
Cephalopoda,	Goniatites.—*Sp.*	133.
	Orthoceras sulcatum.—*Fleming,*	167.

Shale under the Gair or Arden Limestone.

Brachiopoda,	Athyris ambigua.—*Sow.*	
Pelecypoda,	Nucula gibbosa.—*Fleming,*	} 16.
	Sanguinolites? striatolamellosus.—*De Kon.,*	
Gasteropoda,	Pleurotomaria.—*Sp.*	

Dark Calcareous Band under the Gair or Arden Limestone.

Class, etc.	Name.	Locality Number.
Pisces, . . .	Tristychius minor (spine), . . .	. 149.

Gair, Robroyston, Arden, Calmy, or Dykeneuk Limestone.

Foraminifera,	Valvulina palæotrochus.—*Ehrenberg,* .	. 45.
Brachiopoda,	Productus longispinus.—*Sow.?* .	⎫
	„ punctatus.—*Martin,* . .	⎬ 181.
	„ semireticulatus.—*Martin,* .	⎭

Shale over the Gair, Dykeneuk, Bedlay, or Robroyston Limestone.

Plantæ, . . .	Calamites.—*Sp.*	16
Foraminifera, &c.,	Endothyra ammonoides.—*Brady,*	45.
	„ Bowmani.—*Phillips,*	45.
	„ globolus.—*Eichwald,*	45.
	„ radiata.—*Brady,* .	45.
	Trochammina incerta.—*D'Orb.*	45.
	Valvulina palæotrochus.—*Ehrenb.*	. 45.
	„ decurrens.—*Brady,* . .	7.
	Palæocoryne.—*Sp.* . . .	. 128, 129, 130,
Echinodermata,	Hydreionocrinus? globularis.—*De Kon.?*	. 128.
	Archæocidaris (spines, &c.), .	. 7, 9, 45.
Annelida,	Ortonia carbonaria.—*Young,* .	⎰ 128, 129, 130,
		⎱ 183a.
	Serpulites.—*Sp.* . .	17.
	Spirorbis caperatus.—*M'Coy,* .	129.
	„ —*Sp,* . .	181.
Crustacea,	Bairdia curta.—*M'Coy,* . .	45.
	Cythere fabulina.— *J. & K.* .	7.
	Griffithides mesotuberculatus.—*M'Coy,*	45, 181.
	„ mucronata.—*M'Coy,*	9.
	Kirkbya Permiana.—*Jones,* .	45.
	Leperditia Okeni.—*Münster,*	45.
	„ suborbicularis.—*Münster,* .	46.
Polyzoa, .	Diastopora megastoma,—*M'Coy,* .	9, 45, 129,
	Fenestella bicellulata.—*Eth. jun.?*	9.
	Glauconome.—*Sp.* . .	129, 130.
	Goniocladia cellulifera.—*Eth. jun.*	. 128, 129, 130,
	Rhombopora? interporosa.—*Phill.*	. 9.
	Synocladia carbonaria.—*Eth. jun.*	9.
	Thamniscus pustulata.—*Eth. jun.*	. 129, 130.
Brachiopoda, .	Athyris ambigua.—*Sow.* .	⎰ 7, 4, 18,
		⎱ 129,130,183a.
	Chonetes Buchiana.—*De Koninck?*	. 125.
		⎧ 45, 128, 129,
	„ Laguessiana—*De Koninck?* .	⎨ 130, 177, 181,
		⎩ 183a.
	Discina nitida.—*Phillips,* .	. 7, 9, 45, 165,
	Lingula mytiloides.—*Sow.* .	. 7, 45.
	Orthis Michelini.—*Léveillé?*	183a.
		⎰ 7, 16,45, 128,
	„ resupinata.—*Martin,*	⎱ 129, 130.
		⎰ 9, 15, 16, 17,
	Orthotetes crenistria.—*Phillips,* .	⎱ 45, 130, 183.
	Productus latissimus.—*Sow.* .	. 45, 183.
	„ longispinus.—*Sow.* .	. 9.
	„ giganteus.— *Martin,* var.	. 9.
	„ semireticulatus.—*Martin,* .	7? 128, 166,
	Spirifera lineata.—*Martin?* . .	. 9.
		⎰ 7. 45, 128,
	„ trigonalis, *var* bisulcata.—*Sow.*	⎱ 181.
	„ Urei.—*Fleming?* . .	. 128.
	Spiriferina cristata.—*Schlotheim,* .	⎰ 7, 17, 128,
		⎱ 129.
	Strophomena analogn, *var.* distorta, .	. 45,

Class, etc.	Name.	Locality Number.
Pelecypoda,	Aviculopecten ornatus.—*Eth. jun.*	15.
	Cardiomorpha oblonga.—*Sow.* ?	45.
	Cypricardia ? parallela.—*Phillips ?*	7.
	Modiola lithodomoides.—*Eth. jun.*	9.
	Myalina (small.—*Sp.*),	9.
	Nucula gibbosa.—*Fleming,*	7, 45, 128, 129, 181.
	Nuculana attenuata. *Fleming,*	7, 16, 45, 128, 165.
	Pteronites angustatus.—*M'Coy ?*	9.
Gasteropoda,	Bellerophon decussatus.—*Fleming,*	123, 128, 130.
	,, Urei.—*Fleming,*	7, 9, 16, 123, 128, 129, 130.
	,, hiulcus,—*Martin ?*	7. 130,
	Loxonema scalaroidea.—*Phillips ?*	130, 183,
	Naticopsis liratus.—*Phillips,*	129.
	Pleurotomaria atomaria.—*Phillips ?*	7, 128, 129.
	,, contraria.—*De Kon.*	7.
Pteropoda,	Conularia quadrisulcata.—*Sow.*	129.
Cephalopoda,	Cyrtoceras unguis.—*Phill.*	128.
	Goniatites,—*Sp.*	7.
	Nautilus nodosus.—*Armstrong,*	128.
	Orthoceras sulcatum.—*Fleming,*	45.
Pisces,	Rhizodopsis (scales),	19.

Shale in connection with Bedlay Limestone.

Crustacea,	Griffithides mesotuberculatus.—*M'Coy,*	
Brachiopoda,	Chonetes Laguessiana.—*De Kon.*	
	Discina nitida.—*Phillips,*	
	Lingula mytiloides.—*Phillips,*	
	Orthis resupinata.—*Martin,*	
	Orthotetes crenistria.—*Phillips,*	108.
	Productus semireticulatus *var.* pugilis,	
	Spirifera trigonalis.—*Martin,*	
Pelecypoda,	Nuculana attenuata.—*Fleming,*	
Gasteropoda,	Bellerophron Urei.—*Fleming,*	
Cephalopoda,	Discites quadratus.—*Fleming,*	
	Nautilus nodosus.—*Armstrong,*	

Shale on a 6 in. Coal between Gair and Castlecary Limestones.

Foraminifera,	Endothyra globolus.—*Eichwald ?*	
	,, radiata.—*Brady,*	
Echinodermata,	Archæocidaris (spines, plates, &c.),	
Crustacea,	Griffithides (pygidium),	
Brachiopoda,	Orthis Michelini.—*Léveillé,*	8.
	Orthotetes orenistria.—*Phillips,*	
	Productus latissimus.—*Sow.*	
	,, longispinus.—*Sow.*	
	Spirifera trigonalis.—*Martin, var.*	
Pelecypoda,	Schizodus.—*Sp.*	

Thin Limestone between Gair and Castlecary Limestones.

Brachiopoda,	Lingula squamiformis.—*Phill.*	
	Orthotetes crenistria.—*Phillips,*	183.
	Productus semireticulatus.—*Martin ?*	
Pelecypoda,	Posidonomya.—*Sp.*	

Shale above foregoing Limestone.

Foraminifera,	Endothyra Bowmani.—*Phillips,*	
Crustacea,	Bairdia curta.—*M'Coy ?*	
	,, grandis.—*J. & K.*	
	,, rigida.—*Jones,*	
	Beyrichia bituberculata.—*M'Coy,*	8.
	Cythere cuneola.—*J. & K.*	
	,, striolata,	
	Kirkbya annectens.—*J. & K.*	
	,, Permiana.—*Jones,*	

Class, etc.	Name.	Locality Number,
Crustacea,	Leperditia suborbicularis.—*Münster*,	
Brachiopoda,	Chonetes Buchiana.—*De Kon.* (young of ?)	
	Discina nitida.—*Phillips*,	
	Orthis resupinata.—*Martin*,	
	Orthotetes crenistria.—*Phillips*,	
	Productus giganteus.—*Martin, var.*	
	,, latissimus.—*Sow.*	8.
	,, longispinus—*Sow.*	
	,, semireticulatus.—*Martin*,	
	Spirifera lineata.—*Martin*,	
Pelecypoda,	Nuculana attenuata.—*Fleming*,	
Gasteropoda,	Bellerophon decussatus.—*Fleming*,	
	,, Urei.—*Fleming*,	
	Euomphalus carbonarius.—*Sow.*	

Sandstone under Bowdenhill, Castlecary, or Levenseat Limestone.

Plantæ,	Stigmaria,	18.

Castlecary, Levenseat, or Bowdenhill Limestone.

Foraminifera,	Lituola Bennieana.—*Brady*,	42.
	Valvulina palæotrochus.—*Ehrenb.*	42, 43.
Annelida,	Serpulites.—*Sp.*	120.
Crustacea,	Bairdia ampla.—*Reuss*,	43.
	,, elongata.—*Münster*,	42.
	,, plebeia.—*Reuss*,	42, 43.
	Cythere fabulina, *J. & K.*	42.
	,, intermedia ?	
	Griffithides.—*Sp.*	196.
	Leperditia Okeni.—*Münster*,	42.
	,, suborbicularis,	42
Brachiopoda,	Athyris ambigua.—*Sow.*	109a.
	Discina nitida.—*Phillips*,	120.
	Chonetes Laguessiana.—*De Kon.?*	176.
	Orthis resupinata.—*Martin*,	120.
	,, Michelini.—*Léveillé*,	43.
	Orthotetes crenistria.—*Phillips*,	109, 109a.
	Productus longispinus.—*Sow.*	120.
	,, punctatus.—*Martin*,	109a, 120.
	,, scabriculus.—*Martin*,	109a.
	,, semireticulatus.—*Martin*,	109, 109a, 120.
	,, ,, var. Martini,	178.
	Rhynchonella pugnus.—*Martin*,	120.
	Spirifera lineata.—*Martin*,	109a, 176, 178?
	,, trigonalis.— ,,	109, 109a, 120.
Pelecypoda,	Aviculopecten interstitialis.—*Phillips?*.	109a.
Cephalopoda,	Nautilus ingens.—*Martin*,	43.
	,, nodiferus.—*Armstrong*,	109a.
Pisces,	Tomodus convexus.—*Ag.*	43.

Oil Shale over Levenseat Limestone.

Pisces,	Megalichthys (scales),	29.

Shales over Levenseat, Castlecary, or Craigenbuck Limestone.

Actinozoa,	Chætetes.—*Sp.*	29.
Annelida,	Spirorbis.—*Sp.*	29.
Crustacea,	Beyrichia arcuata.—*Bean*,	43.
	Phillipsia.—*Sp.*	29.
Brachiopoda,	Athyris ambigua.—*Sow.*	198.
	Discina nitida.—*Phillips*,	198.
	Lingula mytiloides.—*Sow.*	198, 199.
	Orthis Michelini.—*Léveillé*,	29.
	,, resupinata.—*Martin* ?	13.
	Orthotetes crenistria.—*Phillips*,	13, 199.
	Productus cora.—*D'Orbigny*,	176.
	,, semireticulatus.—*Martin*,	29, 198.
	,, Youngianus.—*Dav.* ?	176.

Class, etc.	Name.	Locality Number.
Brachiopoda, .	Spirifera trigonalis, *var.* bisulcata ? .	176.
	Strophomena analoga.—*Phill.*, . .	29.
Pelecypoda, .	Nuculana attenuata.—*Fleming*, .	198.
	Posidonomya.—*Sp.* .	176.
	Schizodus.—*Sp.*, . . .	198, 199.
Gasteropoda, .	Bellerophon decussatus—*Fleming*, .	198.
	,, Urei.—*Fleming*, .	198.
	Dentalium ingens.—*De Koninck ?*	198.
Pisces, .	Eurynotus crenatus.—*Agass.* (scales), .	43.
	Megalichthys (scales), . .	10.
	Rhizodopsis (scales, &c.), . .	10, 11.

Limestones of doubtful position.

Brachiopoda, .	Orthotetes crenistria.—*Phillips*, .	156.
	Productus semireticulatus.—*Martin*, .	156.
	,, Youngianus.—*Dav. ?* .	147.
	Spirifera trigonalis.—*Martin*, .	147.
Pelecypoda, .	Entolium Sowerbii.—*M'Coy*, .	156.
Gasteropoda, .	Bellerophon Urei.—*Fleming*, .	156.
Cephalopoda, .	Actinoceras giganteum.—*Sow.* .	156.

Shales of Upper Limestone Group of doubtful position.

Brachiopoda, .	Productus longispinus.—*Sow.* .	156.
	,, semireticulatus.—*Martin*, .	179.
	Spirifera Urei.—*Fleming*, .	179.
	Terebratula sacculus.—*Martin*, var.	156.
Pelecypoda,	Leptodomus costellatus.—*M'Coy*, .	156.
	Nucula gibbosa.—*Fleming*, .	156, 176.
	Nuculana attenuata, ,, .	179.
	Posidonomya corrugata.—*Eth. ?* .	156.
Gasteropoda,	Bellerophon Urei.—*Fleming*, .	179.
Pteropoda, .	Conularia quadrisulcata.—*Sow.* .	156.
Cephalopoda, .	Orthoceras sulcatum.—*Fleming*, .	156.

Millstone Grit.

Impure Limestone and Shale under the Curly Ironstone.

Annelida, .	Serpulites carbonarius.—*M'Coy*, . .	
Brachiopoda, .	Discina nitida.—*Phillips*, . .	
	Orthis.—*Sp.* . .	} 46
	Orthotetes crenistria.—*Phillips*, .	
Pelecypoda,	Schizodus.—*Sp.* . .	
Gasteropoda, .	Bellerophon decussatus.—*Fleming*, .	
	Natica variata.—*Phillips ?* . .	

Shale over a Cement Stone in Fireclay.

Brachiopoda, .	Lingula mytiloides.—*Sow.* .	
	Orthotetes crenistria.—*Phillips*, .	} 110.
Pelecypoda, .	Nuculana attenuata.—*Fleming*, .	
	Schizodus (*Sp.* near S. orbicularis.—*M'Coy*), .	

Coal Measures.

Maggie Shale, on Benhar Slatyband Ironstone.

Plantæ, .	Alethopteris lonchitica.—*Schl.*, var. .	55.
	Lepidodendron (fragments), .	55, 56.
	Lepidostrobus (single cones), .	55.
	Lepidophyllum, . .	55.
	Asterophyllites ?—*Sp.* .	55.
Brachiopoda, .	Discina nitida.—*Phillips*, .	55, 56.
	Lingula mytiloides.—*Sow.* .	55.
Annelida,	Serpulites carbonarius.—*M'Coy*, .	53, 55, 56.
	Eurypterus.—*Sp.* (fragments), .	55.

Class, etc.	Name.	Locality Number.
Gasteropoda,	Bellerophon dicussatus.—*Flem.*	55.
	„ Urei.—*Flem.*	55.
Pteropoda,	Conularia quadrisulcata.—*Sow.*	53, 55.
Pisces,	Amphicentrum (plates, &c.),	53.
	Cœlacanthus lepturus.—*Ag.* (plates, &c.),	55, 56.
	Elonichthys Egertoni.—*Agassiz,*	55.
	„ (l. jaw, &c.),	53, 55.
	Mesolepis (scales),	55.
	Megalichthys (scales),	55.
	Rhadinichthys Monensis.—*Agassiz,*	56.
	Rhizodopsis (opercular, &c.),	55, 56.

Blackband Ironstone below Boghead Parrot Coal.—(Torbane-hill Mineral).

Annelida,	Serpula Torbanensis.—*Sp. nov.*	49, 50.
Pelecypoda,	Anthracoptera ? (small sp.),	49, 50.

Boghead Parrot Coal.—(Torbane-hill Mineral).

Plantæ,	Stigmaria,	49, 50.

Blackband Ironstone above Boghead Parrot Coal.

Annelida,	Serpula Torbanensis.—*Sp. nov.*	47.
	Anthracoptera ? (small *Sp.*),	47.

Shale in connection with Auchingane Coal.—(Slamannan District).

Crustacea,	Beyrichia arcuata.—*Bean.*	217.
Pisces,	Megalichthys (scales, teeth),	217.

Shotts Upper Cannel or Gas Coal.

Annelida,	Spirorbis carbonarius.—*Murch. ?*	
Pelecypoda,	Anthracoptera ?—*Sp.*	
Pisces,	Megalichthys (scales),	} 48.
	Rhizodopsis (scales),	
	Strepsodus (scales),	48, 66.

Thin band of Ironstone in Shotts Gas Coal.

Pelecypoda,	Anthracosia acuta.—*Sow.?*	
	New Myaliniform Shell ?	} 66.

Shale above Wee or Lower Drumgray Coal.

Pelecypoda,	Anthracosia robusta.—*Sow.*	79.

Arenaceous Shales in connection with Coxroad Coal.—(Lower Drumgray Coal.)

Plantæ,	Antholites Pitcairniæ.—*L. & H.,*	
	Cordaites (leaves),	
	Neuropteris heterophylla.—*Brong.?*	} 223.
	Sphenopteris (near S. latifolia.—*Brong.*),	

Cleugh Glen Alum Shale, near horizon of Coxroad Coal.

Plantæ,	Alethopteris lonchitica.—*Schl.,* var.	
	Antholites Pitcairniæ.—*L. & H.*	
	Calamites (stems),	
	Cordaites (leaves),	} 210.
	Cyclopteris (pinnulæ),	
	Neuropteris.—*Sp.,*	
	Sphenopteris (near S. acutifolia.—*Brong.*)	

Shale under Coxroad or Upper Drumgray Coal.

Plantæ,	Sphenopteris (near S. latifolia.—*Brong.*),	227.

Shotts Furnace, Upper Drumgray, or Ball Coal.

Class, etc.	Name.	Locality Number.
Plantæ, . . .	Stigmaria, ...	47.
Annelida, . .	Spirorbis, ...	
Pelecypoda, .	Anthracoptera.—Sp.	
	Anthracosia robusta.—Sow., . . .	
Pisces, . .	Amphicentrum granulosum.—Young, .	} 52.
	Cœlacanthus lepturus.—Ag. (scales), .	
	Megalichthys (teeth, &c.), . . .	
	Rhizodopsis (scales, &c.), . . .	
	Strepsodus (teeth, &c.), ...	

Shales overlying Upper Drumgray Coal.

Plantæ, . . .	Asterophyllites (near A. æquisetiformis or A. foliosa),	} 79.
	Calamites.—Sp.; Cyclopteris.—Sp.; and Neuropteris.—Sp.	} 211.
	Lepidostrobus, ...	54, 57, 65.
	Sporangia, ...	58.
Annelida, . .	Spirorbis.—Sp.	54, 57.
Crustacea, . .	Beyrichia arcuata.—Bean. . . .	54, 57, 65.
	Leperditia (obscure Sp.), . . .	57.
Pelecypoda, .	Anthracosia robusta.—Sow. . . .	57.
Pisces, . . .	Cœlacanthus lepturus.—Agass. . .	65.
	,, (remains of), . . .	57.
	Megalichthys coccolepsis.—Young, .	57.
	,, Hibberti.—Agassis, .	{ 54, 57, 58, 59, { 65.
	,, pygmæus.—Traquair (MS.),	57.
	Pleuracanthus lævissimus.—Agass. .	57.
	Pleurodus affinis.—Agass. . . .	57, 59, 65.
	,, Rankini.—Agass. . .	57, 58.

Speckled Ironstone or Ball Coal.

Plantæ, . . .	Stigmaria and Lepidodendron, . . .	47.

Musselband Ironstone near Upper Drumgray Coal.

Plantæ, . .	Calamites and Lepidodendron, . . .	
Crustacea, .	Beyrichia arcuata.—Bean, . . .	} 57.
	Cythere fabulina.—Jones, . . .	

Shale over Kiltongue Coal.

Plantæ, . .	Cordaites (leaves), ...	
	Neuropteris and Sphenopteris, . .	} 97.
Pelecypoda, .	Anthracoptera.—Sp.	

Calcareous Sandstone, 6 ft. above Calderbank Ironstone?

Pelecypoda, . .	Anthracosia robusta.—Sowerby (peculiar variety), ...	} 105.

Shale forming Pavement of Virtuewell Coal.

Plantæ, .	Alethopteris lonchitica.—Schl. . .	
	Neuropteris Loshii.—Brong. ? . .	
	Pecopteris (near P. laciniata, L. & H.),	} 111.
	Sphenopteris (near S. dilatata or S. adiantoides),	
Annelida,	Serpulites.—Sp.	

Shales and Bituminous Bands over the Virtuewell Coal.

Plantæ, . .	Alethopteris lonchitica.—Schl. . .	71, 120a.
	Asterophyllites.—Sp. . . .	71, 120a, 124.
	Calamites.—Sp.	73.
	Lepidodendron.—Sp.	120a.

Class, etc.	Name.	Locality Number.
Annelida,	Spirorbis carbonarius.—*Murchison,*	70.
Crustacea,	Carbonia.—*Sp.*	73.
	Cythere fabulina.—*Jones,*	78.
	Leperditia (small *Sp.*),	73, 78.
Pelecypoda,	Anthracoptera.—*Sp.*	73.
	Anthracosia robusta.—*Sow.* ?	73.
Pisces,	Amphicentrum granulosum.—*Young,*	62.
	Chomatodus (teeth),	62, 68.
	Cœlacanthus lepturus.—*Agass.*	71.
	,, (scales, &c.),	64, 72, 73, 80.
	Ctenodus (scales),	64.
	Ctenoptychius lateralis.—*Barkas,*	64.
	Megalichthys Hibberti.—*Ag.* (teeth, &c.),	{ 62, 64, 68, 75, 80.
	,, pygmæus.—*Traquair (MS.*),	72.
	Orthacanthus cylindricus.—*Agass.*	73.
	Platysomus (scales),	73.
	Pleurodus affinis.—*Agass.*	72.
	Pleuracanthus gibbosus.—*Agass.*	72.
	,, (spine),	62, 73.
	Rhizodopsis (scales),	{ 62, 64, 68, 72, 73.
	Strepsodus (scales, teeth, &c.),	62, 73.
Reptilia,	Loxomma tooth (?),	87.

Airdrie Blackband Ironstone.

Crustacea,	Anthrapalæmon (part of carapace),	87.
	Leperditia (small and obscure),	100.
Pisces,	Megalichthys (scales, &c.),	87, 100.

Coaly Band over Airdrie Blackband Ironstone.

Annelida,	Spirorbis carbonarius.—*Murch.* ?	} 88.
Pisces,	Megalichthys (scales, &c.),	

Shales over Airdrie Blackband Ironstone.

Annelida,	Spirorbis carbonarius.—*Murch.*	} 100.
Pelecypoda,	Anthracoptera.—*Sp.*	

Shales over Virgin Coal.

Plantæ,	Asterophyllites.—*Sp.* Calamites.—*Sp.*	} 122.
	Lepidodendron.—*Sp.* Pecopteris.—*Sp.*	
Pelecypoda,	Anthracoptera.—*Sp.*	

Shales under Splint Coal.

Plantæ,	Alethopteris lonchitica.—*Schl.*	229.
	Asterophyllites.—*Sp.* Calamites.—*Sp.*	107.
	Neuropteris (near N. flexuosa, *Sternb.*, or N. gigantea, *Sternb.*	} 229.
	Neuropteris (near N. gigantea, *Sternb.*, or N. heterophylla, *Brong.*	} 106.
	Neuropteris (near N. Loshii, *Br.*, or N. heterophylla, *Brong.*	} 107.
	Neuropteris (small *Sp.*),	106.
	Sphenopteris (near S. latifolia, *Brong.*),	207.
	Sporangia,	229.

Splint Coal.

Plantæ,	Sporangia,	228.

Roof of Splint Coal.

Plantæ,	Asterophyllites (near A. foliosa.—*L. & H.*),	102.
	,, (near A. tuberculata.—*Sternb.*	102.

Class, etc.	Name.	Locality Number.
Pelecypoda, : .	Anthracosia robusta.—Sow. ?	102.
Pisces, . . ,	Gyracanthus tuberculatus.—Agass.	114, 118.

Shäles, &c., on Splint Coal.

Plantæ, . . ,	Alethopteris lonchitica.—Schl. . . ;	83, 207.
	Antholites Pitcairnæ.—L. & H. ? . .	207.
	Calamites,—Sp. . . . : .	201, 228.
	Lepidodendron (L. Sternbergii, Brong., or L. aculeatum, Sternb.)	} 207, 228.
	Neuropteris (N. Loshii, Brong., or N. heterophylla, Brong.)	} 121.
	,, (N. flexuosa, Sternb., or N. gigantea, Sternb. ?)	} 207.
	Sporangia, ...	228.
Crustacea,	Beyrichia arcuata.—Bean.	201.
Pelecypoda, . ,	Anthracoptera.—Sp. . . .	213, 224.
	Anthracosia robusta.—Sow. . .	201, 219.
Pisces, . . ,	Acanthodes Wardi.—Agassiz. . .	230.
	Acanthodopsis (part of jaw), . .	207.
	Amphicentrum granulosum.—Young, .	207.
	Cœlacanthus lepturus.—Agass. (scales, &c.),	} 204, 207, 219, 228.
	Ctenodus (scales), ...	204, 207, 228.
	Gyracanthus tuberculatus.—Agass. . ,	83.
	Helodus.—Sp.	230.
	Megalichthys (scales, &c.), . .	} 83, 204, 207, 219.
	Pleuracanthus gibbosus.—Agass. : :	204, 207, 219.
	,, (spine), . .	224.
	Pleurodus affinis.—Agass. . .	207, 219, 230.
	Platysomus (scales), . . .	219.
	Rhadinichthys Monensis.—Agass. .	219.
	,, Wardi.—Egerton, .	207.
	Rhizodopsis sauroides (scales, plates, &c.), .	} 83, 84, 207, 219,224,230.
	Strepsodus (scales, &c.), . . .	207, 219.

Musselband over Splint Coal.

Plantæ, , .	Lepidodendron.—Sp. . . .	214.
Crustacea,	Beyrichia arcuata.—Bean, . .	214.
Pelecypoda, : .	Anthracosia acuta.—Sow. . .	213.
Pisces, . :	Cœlacanthus lepturus.—Agass. .	214.
	Megalichthys.—Sp. . . .	214.

Shale over Humph Coal.

Plantæ, . .	Alethopteris lonchitica.—Schl. .	} 69.
	Lepidodendron.—Sp. . . :	

Roof of Main Coal, and Shale over.

Plantæ, : .	Asterophyllites ? (new form), . .	112.
	Calamites, : . . .	118.
	Neuropteris (near N. Loshii.—Brong.) :	112.
	,, (near N. flexuosa, Sternb., or N. heterophylla.—Brong.) . :	} 112.
	Sternbergia, ...	118.
	Stigmaria, ...	118.
Pelecypoda, . :	Anthracomya.—Sp. (? n. Sp. near A. curta.—Brown), . . . :	} 114.

Shale over the Ell Coal.

Plantæ, . .	Alethopteris lonchitica.—Schl. .	112.
	Cyclopteris (?).—Sp. . . .	112.
	Pecopteris.—Sp. . . , .	112.

Class, etc.	Name.	Locality Number:
Plantœ; . .	Sphenopteris (near S. dilatata.—*L. & H.*)	112, 119:
	Trigonocarpum (?);	112.
Annelida,	Spirorbis carbonarius.—*Murch.* .	112.

Palacecraig Ironstone.

Plantœ, :	Calamites.—2 *Sp.* . . . . . ⎫	
	Lepidodendron.—*Sp.* . . . ⎬ 104.	
	Lepidostrobus.—*Sp.* . . . ⎭	
Crustacea;	Leperditia Scotoburdigalensis.—*Hib.?* . .	
	Prestwichia.—*Sp.*	103:
Pelecypoda,	Anthracoptera.—*Sp.*	104.
Pisces, .	Ctenodus (scales), ...	104.
	Megalichthys Hibberti, *Agass.* (jaw, &c.); :	103, 104:
	,, (scales, &c.) . . .	103:
	Pleuracanthus gibbosus.—*Agass.*	104.

Shale over Palacecraig Ironstone.

Plantœ, .	Lepidodendron and Lepidostrobus,	103.
Crustacea,	Estheria tenella.—*Jordan*, . .	102.
Pelecypoda,	Anthracosia (crushed examples), .	103:
Pisces, :	Acanthodes Wardi.—*Agass.* .	103.
	Cœlacanthus (scales), . .	102.
	Elonichthys Egertoni.—*Agass.* .	103.
	Helodus.—*Sp.* (single teeth), .	102.
	Megalichthys Hibberti.—*Agass.* .	102, 103:
	Pleuracanthus gibbosus.—*Agass.* .	103:
	Rhadinichthys.—*Sp.* . . .	102.
	Rhizodopsis sauroides (scales), .	103.
	Strepsodus sauroides (scales), .	102.

Shales, Oil Shales, Ironstones, and other Beds of doubtful position (Coal Measures).

Plantœ, .	Alethopteris lonchitica.—*Schl.* . ⎰ 61, 90, 116, ⎱ 189.	
	Antholites.—*Sp.*, .	85.
	Asterophyllites.—*Sp.* . .	77, 117.
	Calamites.—*Sps.* . ⎰ 82, 116, 117, ⎱ 189, 216.	
	Lepidodendron.—*Sps.* . . .	77, 184, 100.
	Lepidophyllum intermedium.—*L. & H.* .	61, 205.
	Neuropteris.—*Sp.* . . .	216.
	,, (near Loshii, *Br.*, or N. hetero- ⎰ 82, 115. phylla), . . . ⎱	
	Sphenopteris (near S. elegans.—*Brong.*) .	115.
	,, (near S. latifolia), . .	90.
	,, *Sp.* . . .	46.
	Sporangia, ...	95, 218.
Annelida,	Spirorbis carbonarius.—*Murch.* . .	117.
	,, *Sps.* . . . . ⎰ 60, 82, 190 ⎱ 225.	
Crustacea,	Anthrapalæmon.—*Sp.* (portion of carapace),	221.
	Beyrichia arcuata.—*Bean*, . . . ⎰ 79, 184, 188, ⎱ 190.	
	Cythere fabulina.—*Jones?* . .	188, 225.
	Estheria tenella.—*Jordan*, . .	85, 94.
Brachiopoda, .	Lingula squamiformis.—*Phillips*, .	181.
Pelecypoda, .	Anthracomya.—*n. Sp.?* . .	225.
	Anthracoptera (near A. carinta.—*Sow.*), .	115.
	,, (near A. quadrata.—*Sow.*), .	117.
	,, *Sps.*	77, 79, 96.
	Anthracosia acuta.—*Sow.* . . ⎰ 74?, 76?, 79?, ⎱ 115?.	
	,, robusta.—*Sow.* . ⎰ 60, 74, 184?, ⎱ 190?	
	,, *Sps.* .	98, 101, 191.

Class, etc.	Name.	Locality Number.
Pisces, . . .	Cœlacanthus (scales), ...	84.
	Elonichthys Egertoni.—*Agassiz*,	208.
	Gyracanthus tuberculatus.—*Agassiz*, .	96.
	Helodus ? (single teeth), . . .	75.
	Megalichthys (scales, teeth, &c.),	74, 77, 84, 99, 184, 188, 206, 221.
	Platysomus (scales), . . .	184.
	Pleurodus affinis.—*Agassiz*,	75, 205.
	Rhizodopsis (scales, &c.), . .	84, 206.
	Stepsodus sauroides (scales, &c.) . .	116, 184, 188, 208.

Marine Ironstone and Shale near base of Coal Measures.

Planiæ, . .	Lepidophyllum, . . .	67.
Brachiopoda, .	Lingula mytiloides.—*Sow.* .	67, 215.
	„ squamiformis.—*Phill.?* .	215.
	Productus longispinus.—*Sow.* .	215.
Pelecypoda,	Modiola ?—*Sp.* . . .	67.
	Schizodus ? (small obscure sp.), .	67, 215.
Gasteropoda, .	Loxonema or Murchisonia.—*Sp.* .	63, 67.
Pteropoda,	Conularia (fragment), . . .	215.

Post Tertiary—Marine Series.

Carse Clays.

Pelecypoda,	Cardium edule.—*Linn.* (young of), .	202, 203.
	Corbula gibba.—*Olivi.* . .	202.
	Scrobicularia piperata, *Bellon.* .	202, 203.
	Tellina Balthica.—*Linn.* . .	202, 203.
Gasteropoda, .	Littorina litorea.—*Linn.* .	202, 203.
	„ obtusata „ .	203.
	„ rudis.—*Maton*, var. ? .	202.

(*N.B.*—We are indebted to Professor T. Rupert Jones, F.R.S., Mr H. B. Brady, F.R.S., and Dr R. H. Traquair, F.G.S., for assistance in determining species in their respective departments.)

III.—NOTES ON SOME OF THE SPECIES.

CLASS ANNELIDA.

Genus Serpula.

Serpula Torbanensis.—*Sp. nov.*

Sp. char.—Tube elongate, either folded upon itself into a more or less oval loosely arranged coil, or many times convoluted and twisted in an irregular manner, but always with a tendency to assume the former condition; coils sometimes piling towards the centre; section probably circular, or the tubes may have been a little angular—surface longitudinally wrinkled—size of the coils from 1½ to 3 lines in diameter.

Obs.—I cannot refer this form to any of the Carboniferous Annelids with which I am acquainted. Although exceedingly conspicuous, little can be said in the way of description from the coiled and sometimes contorted manner in which its remains are preserved and converted into carbonate of iron. This has to a certain extent altered the surface markings of the tubes; but it has, on the other hand, rendered its presence in the black ironstone so very conspicuous, that it becomes necessary to, at least, designate the species by a name, more especially as, with the exception of a small Anthracoptraform shell, occasionally seen, the *Serpula* is the prevailing fossil in the ironstone. *S. Torbanensis* occurs in the latter in thousands, at times scattered generally through the matrix, but at others grouped into small clusters of an inch or two in extent. It recalls to us certain of those forms met with in younger rocks, rather than those we are accustomed to meet with in Carboniferous strata. Of the latter it approaches nearest to *Serpula* (*Spirorbis*) *helicteres*, Salter, but is quite distinct.

Loc. Nos. 47, 49, 50.—*Horizon.* Blackband ironstone above and below Boghead parrot coal (Torbane-hill mineral).

Collector—Mr J. Bennie.

CLASS CRUSTACEA.

ORDER TRILOBITA.

Genus Phillipsia.—*Portlock*, 1843.

Phillipsia.—*Sp. ind.*

Obs.—The shale above the Castlecary limestone has yielded the fragmentary remains of a species of *Phillipsia*, a pygidium, a thorax and pygidium united, and a portion of a free cheek without the eye. The state of preservation of the two first named is indifferent, but the free cheek exhibits a highly ornate appearance, covered with a series of small pustules, and a prominent crenulating series round the cavity left by the eye, characters which appear to indicate a species nearly allied to *P. pustulata*, Schlotheim, or *P. seminifera*, Phillips.

Loc. No. 29.—*Horizon.* Shale above the Castlecary or Levenseat Limestone, Upper Carboniferous Limestone Group.

Collector—Mr J. Bennie.

CLASS PELECYPODA.

ORDER OSTRACEA.

Genus Aviculopecten.—*M'Coy.*

Aviculopecten.—*Sp. ind.*

Obs.—Shining impressions of what must have been a distinct and well-marked *Aviculopecten* occur in the roof of the Smithy coal, Edge Coal series of Bo'ness. There is no shelly-matter remaining; indeed, the specimens can scarcely be called casts, but are apparently weak impressions of the interior of the shells. As they are, a close resemblance may be traced to *A. planicostatus*, M'Coy,[1] but with a less marked obliquity of the shell. The ears are short and square, unequal, and concentrically striated, and one at least is provided with radiating striæ. The surface of the impressions is ornamented with from eight to twelve or thirteen broad, flat, inequidistant, smooth radiating ribs, with little separation one from the other. The hinge line was about equal in length to that of *A. planicostatus*, and, like the latter, the shell was obliquely produced towards one side. The material is not sufficient in quantity or state of preservation to enable me to give a more definite diagnosis.

Loc. No. 1.—*Horizon.* Shale forming the roof of the Smithy Coal, Edge Coal Series (= Lower Coal Measures of some writers).

Collector—Mr J. Bennie.

Aviculopecten sub-anisotus.—*Sp. nov.?*

(Compare *A. anisotus*, Phillips, *Geol. York.*, 1836, ii. p. 212, t. 6, f. 22; *A. variabilis*, M'Coy, *Synopsis Carb. Foss. Ireland*, 1844, p. 101, t. 16, f. 7; and *A. depilis*, M'Coy, *loc. cit.*, p. 91, t. 16, f. 11).

Sp. char.—Ovate, or nearly orbicular, slightly produced anteriorly; valve rather flattened. *Left valve*, beak acute, slightly projecting above the hinge line; cardinal margin straight, short; ears small, anterior the largest, slightly pointed, not divided from the body of the shell; posterior ear small, undefined, and very slightly pointed; anterior and posterior margins rounded, the former somewhat produced; ventral margin rounded; surface of the valve, including the ears, covered with fine, close, thread-like imbricating laminæ of growth, with flattened, ill-defined, broad radiating ridges, sometimes visible over the whole valve, at others only towards the ventral margin, and again occasionally entirely absent. *Right valve* more convex than the left, with its anterior ear triangular, deeply divided from the body of the shell by a byssal notch and groove, and ornamented with strong, projecting, scale-like laminæ, and two to four radiating ridges; posterior ear pointed, more definitely so than that of the anterior, but not extending beyond the posterior margin of the valve, and ornamented with fine thread-like lines parallel to the margins; general surface of the valve delicately cancellated by fine, almost microscopic radiating lines, and equally fine concentric imbrications.

Obs.—I describe this as a new species with some hesitation. It may be an already described form, but as I am unable to definitely refer it to any of our British forms, so far as they are known to me, I prefer to provisionally give it a name, rather than run the risk of making an erroneous determination. *A. sub-anisotus* may be compared with *Pecten anisotus*, Phillips, so far as the brief description and unsatisfactory figure of the latter will permit comparison. In both, the valve is produced anteriorly;

---

[1] *Synopsis Carb. Foss. Ireland*, 1844, p. 98, t. 14, f. 6.

F

the anterior ear is deeply divided from the body of the shell, and it is marked with radiating and strong transverse laminæ. The posterior ear is but slightly defined, although not so pointed in *P. anistotus* as in our specimen; the inequality in the two ears of the same valve is equally well marked, and the ornamentation of the shell appears to have been after the same type. Very little has been written about *P. anisotus*, beyond Phillip's two lines of description and Brown's copy;[1] and unfortunately we are unacquainted with the opposite valve of *P. anisotus*. A curious resemblance exists between *A. sub-anisotus* and *Pecten variabilis*, M'Coy, and at the same time an equally curious difference. M'Coy's figure represents two valves on a piece of matrix, with an obliquity towards the anterior side, a triangular deeply-defined anterior ear, marked with strong concentric ridges, and an undefined slightly-pointed posterior ear. These are all characters described above as seen in *P. sub-anisotus;* but in the case of my form on the right valve—whereas Prof. M'Coy's are left valves, or, at all events, whatever value may be given to the terms right and left as applied to *Pectens*, opposite valves to that in which the characters described are to be found in *P. sub-anisotus*. A similar variation also appears to exist in the amount of the anterior obliquity and state of the ornamentation in the two species. Again, the left valve of *A. sub-anisotus* resembles to a certain extent several described species, but not to such an extent as to call for any particular remark. The Survey Collection possesses some very well preserved examples of this form from the Campsie district ; and I think, upon the whole, it will be best to provisionally regard it as new, pending further information concerning the two species I have referred to above. The individuals of *P. sub-anisotus* appear to differ amongst themselves in the amount of the anterior obliquity, the state of preservation of the ornamentation, and the convexity of the right valve. I am not acquainted with the characters of the hinge.

Loc. No. 159.—*Horizon.*—Calcareous band of shale in the Main Limestone.
Collector—Mr A. Macconochie.

ORDER MYTILACEA ?

Genus Anthracoptera.—*Salter.*

Anthracoptera tumida.—Sp. nov.

Sp. char.—Transversely triangular, gibbous, with a strong diagonal ridge dividing the valves into two nearly equal halves ; anterior side well marked, tumid, with a slight byssal notch in the margin at a point almost vertically under the beaks, and more conspicuous in the left valve. Posterior end obliquity truncated; the margin forming with the hinge line an obtuse angle, and occasionally emarginate. Hinge line much less than the length of the shell; postero-ventral margin obtusely rounded. Diagonal ridge and umbonal region very convex, forming the most gibbous part of the shell; the ridge is almost median, but if anything a little anterior. Beaks prominent, widely separated, and raised above the hinge line. Surface ornamented with concentric lines of growth parallel to the margins, occasionally developing into laminæ.

Obs.—*A. tumida* has for its essential characters the great tumidity of the valves, strong and nearly median diagonal ridge, and prominent beaks. The convexity of the shell at once distinguishes it from *A. (Mytilus) triangularis*, Sow.;[2] the more prominently developed anterior end, the more median position of the diagonal ridge, and its more direct course across the valves from *A. (Modiola) carinata*, Sow.,[3] and *A. (Avicula) quadrata*, Sow.[4] The gibbosity of the shell places *A. tumida* nearest to *A. carinata*, Sow. *A.? Browniana*, Salter,[5] is so ill-defined that little can be said about it; but it appears to have a much more emarginate posterior margin, and the latter not in any way obliquely truncated. The general outline of *A. tumida* approaches much nearer to another species of the same genus lately described by me—*A.? obesa.*[6]—but many of the points already indicated will also serve as distinctive ones in this case.

Loc. Nos. 2 and 3.—*Horizon.* Shale above the " Brownstone " portion of the Bo'ness Lower Ironstone—Edge Coal Series.
Collector—Mr J. Bennie.

[1] *Fossil Conchology*, 1849, p. 156.
[2] *Trans. Geol. Soc.* 1840, 2d ser. v. t. 39, f. 16.
[3] *Loc. cit.* f. 15.
[4] *Loc. cit.* f. 17.
[5] *Mems. Geol. Survey, Wigan Memoir* 1862, 2d ed. p. 37, f. 3.
[6] *Quart. Jour. Geol. Soc.* xxxiv. p. 12.

IV.—LIST OF OSTRACODA,

COLLECTED FROM LOCALITIES IN SHEET 23 (ONE-INCH, SCOTLAND).[1]

The numbers refer to the Localities given in the Appendix to Explanation 23,
pp. 49–55.

Carboniferous Limestone Series.

Class, etc.	Name.	Locality Number.
Ostracoda,	Bairdia ampla.—*Reuss*,	4, 37, 247, 259.
	,, ,, var.	247.
	,, brevis.—*J. & K.*	141.
	,, curta.—*M'Coy*,	28 ? 83, 98, 111, 130, 141, 142, 143, 145, 147, 148, 152, 155, 259 ? 260, 279.
	,, elongata.—*Münster*,	28 ? 35, 37, 51, 58, 83, 112, 141, 147, 148, 165, 247, 258, 259, 260.
	,, Hisingeri.—*Münster*,	4 ? 28, 112, 155, 258.
	,, plebeia.—*Reuss*,	28, 35, 37, 55, 58, 111, 112, 124, 129, 130, 142, 147, 247, 258, 259, 260, 279.
	,, ,, ,, var. caudata,	83 ? 111.
	,, ,, ,, var. Neptuni,	155.
	,, subcylindrica.—*Münster*,	260, 279.
	,, n. sp. ?	279.
	Beyrichia arcuata.—*Bean*,	79, 194, 195, 258.
	,, bituberculata.—*M'Coy*,	111.
	,, calliculus.—*Eichw.*	51, 58 ? 148.
	,, multiloba.—*Jones*,	130.
	,, subarcuata.—*Bean*,	79, 132.
	,, radiata.—*J. & K.*	147.
	,, Sp. nov.	35, 51, 148.
	Cythere cornigera.—*J. & K.*	155, 259, 279 ?
	,, cuneola.—*J. & K.*	12 ? 35, 51, 55, 58, 98, 124, 129, 130, 132, 142 ? 147, 148, 152, 153, 154, 155, 247 ? 258, 260, 279 ?
	,, fabulina.—*J. & K.*	12, 119, 129, 130 ? 142 ? 145, 148, 153, 154.
	,, n. sp.	98, 279.
	Cytherella parallela.—*J. & K.*	247.
	,, simplex.—*J. & K.*	35, 145.
	,, Sp.	51, 148, 152, 259.
	Kirkbya annectans.—*J. & K ?*	130.
	,, Permiana.—*Jones*,	51, 141, 147, 155, 247, 258, 279.
	,, ,, ,, var.	145, 147.
	,, Urei.—*Jones*,	35, 51, 58, 145, 148, 153, 154, 155.

[1] See Note, Expl. 23, p. 63. We are indebted to the kindness of Prof. T. Rupert Jones, F.R.S., for the determination of the species.

Class, etc.	Name.	Locality Number.
Ostracoda, . .	Kirkbya *Sp. nov.* . . .	. . 4, 35, 111.
	Leperditia Okeni.—*Münster,*	. { 7, 12, 28, 33, 35, 37, 43, 55, 58, 77, 98, 101, 112, 111, 130, 132, 141, 145, 147, 148 152, 153, 155, 247, 258, 260.
	,, ,, ,, *var.* acuta,	. 51, 55 ?
	,, ,, ,, *var.* Scotoburdi- galensis.—*Hib.*	{ 7, 12, 82 ? 131, 260.
	Leperditia suborbiculata.—*Münster,* .	. { 12, 31, 51, 55, 77, 83, 98, 99, 111, 119, 129, 130, 132, 279.
	Polycope simplex.—*J. & K.* .	. 104, 119.

V.—LIST OF PUBLICATIONS,

REFERRING TO THE GEOLOGY AND PALÆONTOLOGY OF THE DISTRICTS IN-
CLUDED IN SHEET 31 OF THE GEOLOGICAL SURVEY OF SCOTLAND.

1811. On the Coal Formation of Clackmannanshire. Bald. *Mem. Wern. Soc.,* i. 479.

1812. A Geological Account of the Southern District of Stirlingshire, commonly called the Campsie Hills. Imrie. *Mem. Wern. Soc.,* ii. 24.

1815. Notice respecting the Old Silver Mine in Linlithgowshire. Fleming. *Thomson's Ann Phil.,* v. 118.

,, Observations on the Orthoceratites of Scotland. Fleming. *Thomson's Ann. Phil.,* v. 199.

,, On a Bed of Fossil Shells on the Banks of the Forth. Fleming. *Thomson's Ann. Phil.,* v. 118.

1821. Additional Observations on the Coal-fields of Clackmannanshire. Bald. *Mem. Wern. Soc.,* iii. 123.

1824. On the Superficial Strata of the Forth District. Blackadder. *Mem. Wern. Soc.,* i. 424.

1825. On the British Testaceous Annelides. Fleming. *Edinb. Phil. Journ.,* xii. 238. [Description and figures of Dentalium from West Lothian.]

1831. Description of a Fossil Crustaceous Animal (*Eidothea*). Scouler. *Edinb. Jour. of Nat. and Geogr. Science,* iii. 352.

1836. On the Freshwater Limestone of Burdiehouse, in the neighbourhood of Edinburgh, belonging to the Carboniferous Group of Rocks ; with supple-mentary notes on other Freshwater Limestones. Hibbert. *Trans. Roy. Soc., Edinb.,* xiii. 169.

1838. History of British Animals, etc. Fleming. Edinburgh, 8vo. (Contains original descriptions of Bathgate Limestone Fossils.)

1839. On the Carboniferous Formation of the Lower Ward of Lanarkshire. Craig. *Trans. High. Soc.,* vi. 341, new series.

1840. On the Coal Formation of the West of Scotland. Craig. *Brit. Assoc. Rep.* 1840, sect. 89.

1841. On the Boulder Deposits near Glasgow. Craig. *Proc. Geol. Soc.,* iii. 415.

1842. Section of the Lanarkshire Coal-fields. Murray. *Proc. Phil. Soc., Glasgow,* i. 105.

,, Notice of Fossil Plants in the Glasgow Geological Museum. Gourlie. *Proc. Phil. Soc., Glasgow,* i. 105.

1843. Description of some New Species of the Genus Pachyodon. Brown. *Ann. Nat. Hist.,* xii. 390.

1845. Geological Notices of the Parishes in the *New Statistical Account of Scotland.* (Counties of Lanark, Linlithgow, Stirling, and Dumbarton.)

1849. Illustrations of the Fossil Conchology of Great Britain and Ireland, with descriptions and localities of all the species. Brown. London, 4to. Description of a "unio" from Coal-Measures, Polmont, Stirlingshire.

1850. Notice respecting a Deposit of Shells near Borrowstounness. Maclaren. *Edinb. New Phil. Journ.*, xlviii. 311.

,, An Account of the Mineral Field between Airdrie and Bathgate, and from Bathgate to Edinburgh and Leith. Bald. *Edinb. New Phil. Journ.*, xlviii. 173.

1855. On the Geology of Clydesdale. Bryce. (Published for Members of the British Association, 2nd ed. 1859, 3rd ed. 1865. Glasgow, 8vo.

1857. An Investigation into the Structure of the Torbane-hill Mineral, and of various kinds of Coals. Bennett. *Trans. Roy. Soc., Edinb.*, xxi. 173.

1857-62. A Monograph of British Carboniferous Brachiopoda. Davidson. *Mons. Pal. Soc.*, x.-xiv. (Contains much information regarding the Carboniferous Limestone Brachiopoda of the Campsie Hills, etc.)

1859-61. The Carboniferous System in Scotland characterised by its Brachiopoda. Davidson. *Geologist*, ii. p. 461 ; iii. 14, 99, 179, 219, 258. Also published separately.

1860. Observations on the Supply of Coal and Ironstone from the Mineral Fields of the West of Scotland. Moore. *Proc. Phil. Soc., Glasgow*, iv. 292.

,, On the Geology of the Campsie District. Young. *Trans. Glasgow Geol. Soc.*, i. 5. 2d ed. 1868, with alterations and omissions.

1861. On the Chronology of the Trap-rocks of Scotland. Geikie. *Trans. Edinb. Roy. Soc.*, xxii. 633.

,, Memoir to Sheet 32. Geological Survey of Great Britain. Geikie and Salter. London, 8vo.

,, On some of the Higher Crustacea from the British Coal-Measures. Salter. *Quart. Journ. Geol. Soc.*, xvii. 528.

1862. Researches in Newer Pliocene Geology. Smith. Glasgow, 8vo.

,, A Monograph on the Fossil *Estheriæ*. Rupert Jones. *Mons. Pal. Soc.* London, 4to. (Describes species from Sheet 31.)

,, Sketch of the Geology of the Torbane Mineral Field. Taylor. *Geologist*, v. 43.

1863. Glacial Drift of Scotland. Geikie. *Trans. Glasgow Geol. Soc.*, i. pt. 2.

,, Description of *Anthracosaurus Russelli*, a new Labyrinthodont from the Lanarkshire Coal-field. Huxley. *Quart. Jour. Geol. Soc.*, xix. 56.

,, On a new Crustacean from the Glasgow Coal-field. Salter. *Quart. Journ. Geol. Soc.*, xix. 519.

1864. Provisional Notice of a new *Chiton*, and a new species of *Chitonellus*, from the Carboniferous Rocks of Western Scotland. Young and Kirkby. *Trans. Glasgow Geol. Soc.*, ii. 13.

1865. On an undescribed Cone from the Carboniferous Beds of Airdrie. Carruthers. *Geol. Mag.*, ii. p. 433.

,, On the *Tellina Calcarea* Bed of Chapelhall, near Airdrie. Crosskey. *Quar. Journ. Geol. Soc.*, xxi. 219.

1866. Notes on some Fossil Crustacea, etc. Woodward. *Trans. Geol. Soc., Glasgow*, ii. 234.

1867. On the Ballagan Series of Rocks. J. W. Young. *Trans. Glasgow Geol. Soc.*, ii. 209.

,, On the Discovery of Carboniferous Limestone Fossils in the Upper Coal-Measures to the east of Glasgow. Skipsey. *Trans. Glasgow. Geol. Soc.*, ii. 52.

,, On the Age of certain Trap-rocks near Glasgow. Bryce. *Trans. Glasgow Geol. Soc.*, ii. 17.

,, On the Entomostraca of the Carboniferous Rocks of Scotland. Jones and Kirkby. *Trans. Glasgow Geol. Soc.*, ii. 213.

,, On the Range and Occurrence of *Anthracosia* and other Shells in the Coal-Measures eastward of Glasgow. Skipsey. *Trans. Glasgow Geol. Soc.*, ii., 142.

,, Description of two new species of Shells from the Carboniferous Limestone of Clydesdale. Armstrong. *Trans. Glasgow Geol. Soc.*, ii. 74.

1868. Notice of the discovery of *Archæocidaris* with Spines attached. Young. *Proc. Glasgow Nat. Hist. Soc.*, i. 178.

,, On the various Genera and Species of Brachiopod Shells found in the Main Limestone of the Campsie Valley. Young. *Proc. Nat. Hist., Glasgow*, i. 95.

,, On the Gasteropod Mollusca of the Carboniferous Limestones of the West of Scotland. Young. *Proc. Nat. Hist., Glasgow*, i. 70.

1868. On the genera *Heterophyllia* (from the Campsie Hills) *Battersbyia, Palæocylus*, and *Asterosmlia*. Dr Duncan. *Phil. Trans.*, clvii. 648.

1869. Remarks and Notes of Correspondence on the Identity of *Heterophyllia Lyelli* and *H. mirabilis* of Duncan. Young. *Proc. Nat. Hist. Soc., Glasgow*, i. 256.

,, On the Surface Geology of the district round Glasgow, as indicated by the Journals of certain bores. Bennie. *Trans, Glasgow Geol. Soc.*, iii. 133.

,, On Palæocoryne, a genus of Tubularine Hydrozoa from the Carboniferous formations (Campsie Hills). Duncan and Jenkins. *Phil. Trans.*, pp. 159, 693.

1870. On two River Channels buried under Drift, belonging to a period when the land stood several hundred feet higher than at present. Croll. *Trans. Edinb. Gcol. Soc.*, i. 333.

,, On the discovery of a Sand-dyke, or old River Channel, running north and south from near Kirk of Shotts to Wishaw, Lanarkshire. Dick. *Trans. Edinb. Geol. Soc.*, i. 345.

,, On the Bones of a Seal found in red clay near Grangemouth, with remarks on the species. Turner. *Proc. Edinb. Roy. Soc.*, vii. 105.

1871. Observations on the Structure of Fossil Plants found in Carboniferous Strata. Binney. *Mons. Pal. Soc.*, 1871. (Describes new species of *Lepidostrobus* from Airdrie.)

,, The Estuary of the Forth and the adjoining Districts viewed Geologically. Milne Home. Edinburgh, 8vo.

,, On the Upper Coal-Measures of Lanarkshire, Grossart. *Trans. Glasgow Geol. Soc.*, iii. 96.

,, On the Carboniferous Fossils of the West of Scotland—Young; with a General Catalogue of the Fossils—Armstrong. *Trans. Glasgow Geol. Soc.*, iii. Supplement.

,, On the Post-Tertiary Deposits of the Carse of Falkirk. Burns. *Trans. Glasgow Geol. Soc.*, iii. 367.

,, Notes on the Coal-fields at Falkirk, illustrated with and specimens of *Antholites* and its Fruit, *Halonia*, and other Fossil Plants. Peach. *Geol. Mag.*, viii. 187.

1872. Notice of the Geological Features of the Upper Coal-Basin of the Firth of Forth. Cadell. *Trans. Edinb. Geol. Soc.*, ii. 39.

,, Notes on one of the Bathgate Sand-hills. Linn. *Trans. Edinb. Geol. Soc.*, ii. 33.

,, Suggestions for the study of the Chemical Geology of the Bathgate Hills. Taylor. *Trans. Edinb. Geol. Soc.*, ii. 73.

,, A Monograph of the British Fossil Crustacea belonging to the order *Merostomata*. Woodward. *Mons. Pal. Soc.*, xxv., xxvi. (Describes the Bathgate *Eurypterus*.)

1873. On *Antholites Pitcairnæ* and its Fruit (*Cardiocarpum*), with other Fossil Plants from Falkirk. Peach. *Proc. Bot. Soc., Edinburgh*, xi. 108.

,, On Fossil Plants from the Coal-field of Slamannan, Falkirk, etc. Peach. *Proc. Bot. Soc., Edinburgh*, xi. 342.

,, On the Phyllotaxis of *Lepidodendron*. Dickson. *Proc. Bot. Soc., Edinburgh*, xi. 145

,, Memoirs of the Geological Survey of Scotland. Explanation to Sheet 23, p. 42. Edinburgh, 8vo.

,, On some of the less common Bathgate Fossils. Linn. *Trans. Edinb. Geol. Soc.*, ii. 192.

,, On Palæcoryne, etc. Duncan. *Quart. Journ. Geol. Soc.*, xxix. 412.

,, On the Bituminous Shales of Linlithgowshire and Edinburghshire. Taylor. *Trans. Edinb. Geol. Soc.*, iii. 16.

1874. Note on some Fossil Cones from the Airdrie Blackband Ironstone. Panton. *Trans. Edinb. Geol. Soc.*, ii. 307.

,, The Fossils of the Carboniferous Strata of the West of Scotland. No. 1, Robroyston. Young and Armstrong. *Trans. Glasgow Geol. Soc.*, iv. 267.

,, The Carboniferous Entomostraca (Part 1, *Cyprinidæ*). Jones, Kirkby, and Brady. *Mons. Pal. Soc.*, 1874. (Describes species from Bathgate, etc.)

,, On a specimen of *Acanthodes Wardi* (Egerton) from the Lanarkshire Coal-field. Thomson. *Trans. Glasgow Geol. Soc.*, iv. 57.

,, On *Uronemus Magnus*, a new Fossil Fish from the Coal-Measures of Airdrie, Lanarkshire. Traquair. *Geol. Mag.*, 2d Dec., i. 514.

1876. Catalogue of the Western Scottish Fossils. Armstrong, Young, and Robertson; with introduction by Professor Young. Glasgow, 12mo.

,, Contributions to the chief Generic Types of the Palæozoic Corals. Nicholson and Thomson. *Ann. and Mag. Nat. Hist.*, 4th series, xvii. 123, 290.

1876. Notes on *Archæocidaris*, a Carboniferous Echinoderm, with overlapping plates. Young. *Proc. Nat. Hist. Soc., Glasgow*, ii. 225.

,, The Carboniferous and Permian Foraminifera (the genus Fusulina excepted). Brady. *Mons. Pal. Soc.*, 1876.

,, On High Level Terraces in Carron Valley, county of Linlithgow. Milne Home. *Rep. Brit. Assoc.*, 1876, sect. 94.

1877. Note on the genus *Anthrapalæmon* (*Palæocarabus* of Salter) from the Coal-Measures. Woodward. *Geol. Mag.*, 2d Dec.; vol. iv. 55.

,, Further Contributions to British Palæontology. Description of *Fissodus Pattoni*, from Dean Pit, Kinneil, Bo'ness. Etheridge. *Geol. Mag.*, 2d Dec.; vol. iv. 306.

,, On River Débris found in Sandstone. Grossart. *Trans. Geol. Soc., Glasgow*, v. 188.

,, Notes on a Tract of Vertical Trees in Carboniferous Strata. Grossart. *Trans. Geol. Soc., Glasgow*, v. 184.

,, Geological Notes on the Cuttings in the City of Glasgow Union Railway between Bellegrove and Springburn. Neilson. *Trans. Geol. Soc., Glasgow*, v. 222.

LIST OF PUBLICATIONS

OF THE

GEOLOGICAL SURVEY OF SCOTLAND.

I.—Maps on One-inch Scale.

1. Wigtownshire, Southern Districts. 4s.
2. Wigtownshire, South-Eastern Districts. 4s.
3. Wigtownshire, South-Western Districts. 6s.
4. Wigtownshire, East Part: Kirkcudbright, Portion of W. Division. 6s.
7. Ayrshire, South-Western Districts. 6s.
9. Kirkcudbrightshire, N.E.; Dumfriesshire, S.W. 6s.
13. Ayrshire, Turnberry Point. 4s.
14. Ayrshire, Southern Districts. 6s.
15. Dumfriesshire, N.W.; Ayrshire, S.E.; and Lanarkshire, S. corner. 6s.
22. Ayrshire, Northern Districts, and Southern parts of Renfrewshire. 6s.
23. Lanarkshire, Central Districts. 6s.
24. Peeblesshire. 6s.
30. Renfrewshire; parts of Dunbarton, Stirling, Lanark, and Ayr. 6s.
31. Lanarkshire, N.; Stirlingshire, S.; Linlithgowshire, W. 6s.
32 Edinburghshire and Linlithgowshire. 6s.
33. Haddingtonshire. 6s.
34. Eastern Berwickshire. 4s.
40. Fife and Kinross. 6s.
41. Fife, East part. 6s.

II.—Maps on Six-inch Scale, illustrating the Coal-fields.

Edinburghshire.   Sheets 3, 8, 14, 17. 4s.
    ,,   Sheets 2, 6, 7, 12, 13, 18. 6s.
Haddingtonshire. Sheets 8, 13. 4s.
    ,,   Sheets 9, 14. 6s.
Fife.   Sheets 33, 37. 4s.
    ,,   Sheets 24, 25, 30, 31, 32, 35, 36. 6s.
Ayrshire.   Sheets 9, 26, 31. 4s.
    ,,   Sheets 7, 8, 11, 12, 13, 16, 17, 18, 19, 22, 23, 24, 27, 28, 29, 30, 33, 34, 35, 36, 40, 41, 42, 46, 47, 50, 52. 6s.
Renfrewshire. Sheets 13, 14, 17. 4s.
    ,,   Sheets 7, 8, 11, 12, 15, 16. 6s.
Lanarkshire. Sheets 1, 2, 3, 4, 5, 10. 4s.
    ,,   Sheets 6, 7, 8, 9, 11, 12, 13, 16, 17, 18, 19, 20, 23, 24, 25, 31, 32, 37, 38, 41, 42, 49. 6s.
Dumfriesshire. Sheet 1. 4s.
    ,,   Sheets 5, 6, 7. 6s.
Dumbartonshire. Sheets 19A, 20, 24, 26, 28, including 29. 4s.
    ,,   Sheets 23, 25. 6s.
Stirlingshire. Sheets 25, 33, 36. 4s.
    ,,   Sheets 17, 18, 23, 24, 27, 28, 29, 30, 31, 32, 35. 6s.

III.—Horizontal Sections.   5s. per Sheet.

Sheet 1. Edinburghshire and Haddingtonshire.
  ,,   2. Edinburghshire and Haddingtonshire.
  ,,   3. Peeblesshire, Edinburghshire, Linlithgowshire.
  ,,   4. Ayrshire Coal-fields (west side).
  ,,   5. Ayrshire Coal-fields (east side).
  ,,   6. Renfrewshire and Dumbartonshire.
  ,,   7. Cheviot and Lammermoor Hills.
  ,,   8. Clyde Coal-field and Campsie Hills.

V.—Vertical Sections.   3s. 6d. per Sheet.

Sheet 1. Edinburgh Coal-field.
  ,,   3. Kilmarnock Coal-field.
  ,,   4. Clyde Basin Coal-field.
  ,,   5. Stirling and Clackmannan Coal-fields.

V.—Geological Memoirs, to accompany the Sheets of the One-inch Map.

Sheet 1. Wigtownshire, Southern Districts. 3d.
  ,,   2. Wigtownshire, South-Eastern Districts. 3d.
  ,,   3. Wigtownshire, South-Western Districts. 3d.
  ,,   4. Wigtownshire, E. part; Kirkcudbright, portion of W. Division. 9d.
  ,,   7. Ayrshire, South-Western District. 3d.
  ,,   9. Kirkcudbrightshire, N.E.; Dumfriesshire, S.W. 1s.
  ,,   13. Ayrshire, Turnberry Point. 3d.
  ,,   14. Ayrshire, Southern District. 3d.
  ,,   15. Dumfriesshire, N.W.; Ayrshire, S.E.; and Lanarkshire, S. corner. 3d.
  ,,   22. Ayrshire, Northern District, and Southern parts of Renfrewshire. 3d.
  ,,   23. Lanarkshire, Central Districts. 1s.
  ,,   24. Peeblesshire. 3d.
  ,,   31. Lanarkshire, N.; Stirlingshire, S.; Linlithgowshire, W. 2s. 3d.
  ,,   32. Edinburghshire and Linlithgowshire. Out of print. New edition in preparation.
  ,,   33. Haddingtonshire. 2s.
  ,,   34. Eastern Berwickshire. 2s.

A Detailed Catalogue may be had gratis, on application to Messrs W. & A. K. Johnston, 4 St Andrew Square, *Edinburgh ; or to* Messrs Smith & Son, *St Vincent Street, Glasgow.*